CREATE WITH CO-AUTHORS

HOW TO USE EFFECTIVE COLLABORATION TO LEVEL UP YOUR WRITING CAREER

DONNA BARKER   CRYSTAL HUNT
EILEEN COOK

Copyright © 2021 by Donna Barker, Crystal Hunt and Eileen Cook

Published by The Creative Academy for Writers

All rights reserved.

www.creativeacademyforwriters.com

No part of this book may be reproduced in any form or by any electronic or mechanical means, including information storage and retrieval systems, without written permission from the author, except for the use of brief quotations in a book review.

ISBNs

978-1-990220-07-4 (Mobi)

978-1-990220-08-1 (ePub)

978-1-990220-06-7 (Paperback)

978-1-990220-09-8 (Hardcover)

978-1-990220-10-4 (Audiobook)

Although the author and publisher have made every effort to ensure that the information in this book was correct at publication, the author and publisher do not assume and hereby disclaim any liability to any party for any loss, damage or disruption caused by errors or omissions, whether such errors or omissions result from negligence, accidents or any other cause.

CONTENTS

A note about spelling   5
Introduction   9
How to get the most out of this book   11

PART I
WHY CO-AUTHOR SOMETHING?

1. Why do you want to co-author something?   17
2. What are the upsides of co-authoring?   23
3. What are the challenges of co-authoring?   33

PART II
HOW CAN YOU COLLABORATE WITH OTHER AUTHORS?

4. What kind of co-author relationship is right for you?   43
5. Two or more writers writing under one pen name   49
6. Two or more writers writing under their own names   55
7. Headliner and co-author   59
8. Shared-world stories   63
9. Ghostwriting and writing for hire   71
10. Anthologies and boxed sets   75

PART III
WHO WILL YOU WRITE WITH?

11. What is your author goal?   89
12. What should you look for in a co-author?   95
13. What co-author qualities would complement yours?   103
14. What do you need to know about your writing partner?   111
15. Where can you find a writing partner?   117

PART IV
HOW WILL YOU WRITE TOGETHER?

16. What kind of a book are you co-writing?	125
17. How will you write that book?	131
18. What writing tools will you use?	137
19. What commitments are you making?	143
20. How will you ensure consistency and safety of backups?	151
21. How can you share a writing world?	155
22. How do you resolve conflicts in the writing process?	159
23. How much polishing is enough?	165

PART V
HOW WILL YOU HANDLE PUBLICATION?

24. What is your publication goal?	171
25. What is your publication path?	173
26. What form will your shared publishing business take?	177
27. What contracts do you need in place before you get started?	187
28. How will you sell the books?	195
29. How are revenues shared?	201
30. How will you handle taxes?	209
31. How are expenses shared?	215
32. How will you manage shared assets?	225
33. How do agents and editors view co-written books?	227
34. How do you query a co-written book?	231
35. How will you keep things running smoothly?	239
36. How will you handle conflict?	245
37. How and when will you end the partnership?	251
38. How will you deal with success?	259
39. What's next?	263
More Creative Academy Guides for Writers	267
About Donna Barker	269
About Crystal Hunt	271
About Eileen Cook	273
Acknowledgements	275
Resources	277

A note about spelling…

All three of the founding members of The Creative Academy for Writers live in Canada, and we made a conscious decision to use Canadian spellings throughout our series of guides. Because… well… it's who we are, eh?!
A note to our American readers and other friends from around the world: we welcome U in Canada :) Thanks for your willingness to learn new things and play nice with your colourful Canadian neighbours.

While we always appreciate readers letting us know about errors in our books, pretty please double-check Canadian spellings before you tell us we're wrong.

We've left American spellings intact in quoted material.

xo Crystal, Donna and Eileen

We dedicate this book to all the present and future co-authors out there who share so generously of their time, ideas, creative energy and practical skills to help each other be more than we could ever be on our own.

INTRODUCTION

It's a truth universally acknowledged that writing is a solitary activity.

We imagine the artist alone in their garret with a laptop or a pad of paper, crafting a book to make readers thrill, cry or discover something new.

There are hundreds, if not thousands, of jokes about writers—introverts, with only their imaginary friends for company, pounding their heads on the desk until the words and story flow from their fingertips and onto the page.

But what if that image was wrong—or at least not the whole picture? What if writing didn't have to be a solo pursuit? What if it could be done with someone else, kind of like a literary Blue Man Group?

The reality is that co-writing has been around since the publication of the very first books. All the way back to the Bible, writers have come together to tell stories, to share their knowledge and skills, and to increase the number of books they can produce.

Centuries ago, Alexandre Dumas used co-writers to help write his novel *The Three Musketeers* in the same way that James Patterson employs co-authors to increase his output now. Carolyn Keene is listed as the author of the Nancy Drew novels, but that was a pen name for a group of authors who wrote in the world of the girl super sleuth. Modern-day thriller writer Nicci French is the pen name of married couple Nicci Gerrand and Sean French. Stephen King did it with Peter Straub in order to write *The Talisman*. *Good Omens*, which was recently made into an Amazon TV show, was a collaborative writing venture by Neil Gaiman and Terry Pratchett. And the list goes on.

Non-fiction often has co-writers. It's common for two experts to come together to blend their expertise. From *Barbarians at the Gate* by Bryan Burrough and John Helyar to *Freakonomics* by Steven D. Levitt and Stephen J. Dubner. (What are the odds of two people not just writing a book together, but both being named Steve?)

And here's an unexpected shocker, or not—this book, the one you're reading right now, was co-written as well.

Perhaps you've been co-writing for a while, or perhaps you're considering it for the first time. The three of us (Donna, Crystal and Eileen) have all both written books independently and teamed up with other authors. While there are few things better than handing a manuscript over to someone else to tackle when you're struggling, there are also interesting challenges when you write with others.

We've written this book to help you understand the process of co-writing, in particular the tricky bits that you might not anticipate until you're deep into the journey of writing and publication, when it might be uncomfortable to address something in the partnership that's not working quite right.

We've laid out what you need to know to determine whether writing with a co-author is a good fit for you and, if it is, how to make it work.

HOW TO GET THE MOST OUT OF THIS BOOK

You're a grown-up (we assume), and this is your book. Ultimately, you're going to do what you want with it. We respect that.

However, we do have some suggestions about how to get the most from our wise and well-researched words and from the accompanying workbook. It's not because we're bossy. We just appreciate efficiency, and helping writers work smarter, not harder, is kind of our thing.

Like most of our Creative Academy Guides for Writers, we recommend that you read this book through, from top to tail, and flag the sections particularly relevant to your situation. You will likely also want to grab the *Create With Co-Authors* workbook—don't worry, it's free—a fillable Google Doc where you can answer the Your Turn questions in one place. You can download your copy from our website at CreativeAcademyForWriters.com/resources.

Then, we recommend you work through the book a second time. (Yeah, we know you're busy, but trust us here.) Think of it like sitting down to take an exam. First, you scan through the whole test to make sure you're in the right classroom. Then you answer the questions you know—this boosts your confidence for the ones you must think about a little more.

When reading non-fiction teaching books, it's often useful to grasp the big picture, and to make a note of questions and gut reactions on your first read-through—leaving blank those areas you're not sure about.

On your second pass, you'll have deeper context. You may have done some research, talked to other authors, and explored ways to fill in those gaps, section by section, until your *Create With Co-Authors* workbook is complete.

And when it is? You will have a fantabulous co-author plan and draft working agreement to use when you discuss writing a project with another person.

Co-writing *vs.* co-authoring

In this book, we use the terms *co-writing* and *co-authoring* interchangeably. Later we'll discuss different models you can use when working on a project with another writer, but for now, know that when we say *co-write* and *co-author*, we mean the process of sharing responsibility for the creation of a manuscript. And that even when we are using singular co-author, we are referring to any co-writing situation with multiple authors.

Looking for a full-time support system for your journey?

Hanging on to your dream of being an author can be hard. Friends and family may not understand that it can take years, even decades, to build a writing career. Folks who are not writers themselves often don't understand the siren's call of the fresh notebook, the lure of the blank page, the endless possibilities that await you in the worlds you create.

Non-writers don't get it. And that's okay. Because *we do*.

We writers need someone to believe in our dream and boost us up when we feel like letting go. Choosing to write books takes courage. Courage to continue to try when the words won't come. Courage to share your work with others and invite their feedback. Courage to send those words off into the world, through agents and editors or by indie publishing your story.

The bad news is that the world has too many people who will tell you your dream is foolish. Instead of cheering you on, they'll go out of their way to discourage you, because it's easier for them to tear down someone else's dream than to work toward one of their own.

Whether you're writing your first book or fiftieth, we writers need to surround ourselves with the *right* people.

That's why we started The Creative Academy for Writers. We wanted to create an inclusive place that fostered big dreams for writers and gave them the tools, guidance and support to reach those dreams. We wanted to build a community of like-minded people who could support and encourage each other in taking the next steps on their writing journey. We wanted to be that voice in your ear that says "you got this" when you feel like you very much don't.

We hope this book is a part of that journey for you.

If you aren't already a member of The Creative Academy for Writers, we invite you to join us online. You can find us at CreativeAcademyForWriters.com. We have a wide range of both live and recorded events, active forums, guest speakers and scads of support, regardless of where you are on your writing journey. Many of the resources we mention in this book are available to you there.

Membership is free—yes, you read that right—because community is always stronger when it is more diverse.

PART I

WHY CO-AUTHOR SOMETHING?

1

WHY DO YOU WANT TO CO-AUTHOR SOMETHING?

What is your why?

If you're a writer, you've undoubtedly had the experience of being at a party when someone discovers that you're an author. First, they inquire if you've written anything they would have heard about. Then they share how they've often considered writing their own novel, maybe once they retire. By this time, they likely have you pinned against the snack table, unable to escape without "accidentally" tripping into the bowl of chip dip. And that's when they pounce with the dread proposal they're certain will excite you.

"You know what," they declare, eyes wide, "I've got a great idea for a book! How about we do it together? I'll share this winning idea with you, and then you just do the writing bit. Then we can share the profits fifty-fifty."

What typically follows is an awkward conversation—or your hand finding its way into that bowl of dip, requiring you to make a hasty exit from the conversation to the bathroom.

This isn't to suggest that the first baby step of a successful co-writing partnership can't be made at a social event. But this kind of proposal is not one to either be made or entered into like it's a drunken Vegas wedding to an interesting person you've only recently met.

There are a range of good reasons to consider teaming up with another writer. And an equal number of reasons to be careful. Being crystal clear on why you are interested in sharing the load of writing and publishing a book is the first step to making a co-authoring decision you can feel confident about.

Before we get to your "why," we want to share our stories so you can see how things may work and how you can set yourself up for co-authoring success.

Our stories

Eileen's experience with co-writing

Eileen's first experience with co-writing was with a big-five publisher. She was approached by an editor who had seen her work and thought she would be a good fit for a project they were developing in-house. The publisher had an idea for a young adult series, along with character ideas and a loose plot outline.

At this point in her career, Eileen had never done any kind of writing where she wasn't the one who had developed the story, but she was intrigued by the different aspects of the opportunity —the interesting story idea, the chance to work collaboratively with this particular editor, and the chance to earn additional money from a book project. The project had its ups and downs—many of which are discussed in this book—but in the end she wrote a YA series under a pen name. While she enjoyed it, she wasn't sure if she wanted to do it again. It turns out she has strong ideas about characters and plots and doesn't always share well. She blames the fact that she grew up as an only child.

When the team at The Creative Academy for Writers developed the idea for this non-fiction series, it was clear that some of the titles would benefit from being co-written. Eileen discovered that while sharing fiction writing was a challenge for her, she loved melding ideas as part of a non-fiction process. And, assuming that she's still alive at publication, it appears her partners liked working with her too.

Eileen's why: For Eileen, co-writing, especially non-fiction, allows her to expand her ideas. When her co-writers share their experience and knowledge, it allows her to think of things in new ways. From a business perspective, it also allows her to produce more content (and thus more income) in a shorter amount of time.

Donna's experience with co-writing

Donna, on the other hand, has had significantly more experience as a co-author, both credited and not, than as the sole boss of her words.

Her very first co-writing experience was in a university film production course. She partnered with a young woman she'd never spoken to until they found themselves sitting together in class one day. They chatted about the main themes of the short films they were considering writing, producing and directing on their own. Realizing they had very similar visions, they decided to co-write and co-produce a film for the class.

Donna and Suzanne had to make hundreds of creative and financial decisions in the making of that film, sharing not just the writer credit, but director, producer and editor credits, too. Oh, and they were both just 21 years old, doing something that carried the real risk of unfathomable humiliation, since all the films would be screened in a public theatre at the end of the semester.

Did they know what they were signing themselves up for? Not in the least! Did it work out? The film (and filmmakers) were recognized as better than good, they worked on a couple of music videos together after that, and the two maintain a friendship to this day.

That experience set Donna up to trust collaborative writing, and her career was built on projects that had multiple authors. Sometimes she was credited, but often she was not. She was a happy ghost, being paid to do what she loved, even if only two people knew she was a co-author.

Donna's why: Although Donna is now the sole author of five published novels and one novella (as of print time), writing as a co-author for over 20 years served two purposes—it matched her personality and her desire not to be the centre of attention before she had the confidence to declare herself a "real" writer. Being a ghostwriter was a lucrative career for two decades.

Crystal's experience with co-writing

Crystal's experience with co-authors is varied, and she has co-authored a combination of credited and uncredited projects over the past 20 years. She started her publishing career in academics, and academic papers are generally co-written, so when it came to more "artistic" writerly pursuits, it wasn't too much of a stretch to consider collaboration.

Her first foray into fiction was writing picture books for children. Having no illustration skills of her own, collaboration was a no-brainer, and she teamed up with a series of different illustrators.

She has ghostwritten early reader chapter books, where she was provided the plot, language levels and parameters. She has collaboratively written early readers with her husband Jared, where they would brainstorm the idea together, one would draft it and one would flesh out and polish the story. Crystal and Jared used a similar process for several co-written non-fiction titles as well.

It was these early adventures in collaborative writing that made it easier to consider working with other writers for future opportunities like The Creative Academy Guides for Writers and a screenplay for a holiday romance.

Crystal's why: Crystal enjoys co-authoring because of the social connection that comes from working creatively with other people, and because partners can build on each other's ideas and raise things to the next level. It's also really rewarding to share the work, to have someone to celebrate with, and—because she loves to promote other people's work more than her own—to make the marketing side of things easier!

Thinking about your why

When writing believable characters, it's critical to know their motivation. Without a clear and believable motivation, the character will not continue to move toward their goal. You're no different than our imaginary friends. You need to know your motivation.

You may want to co-write because you love working with your partner, or because you're too busy to tackle a full project on your own. You may be interested in the financial benefits of co-authoring a book, or a co-authored book project may speak to your heart.

Your why is a place to check in when things in your writing partnership get difficult. Because—we hate to tell you this—there will be challenges.

The three of us love working together and have a huge amount of respect for each other. However, there are still times when we argue over a point, butt heads on deadlines, or have different ideas about how to promote a project. Knowing *why* we work together gives us focus when we have to work through the difficult conversations.

So, what are the pros and cons of writing with others? We'll dive into that in the next section. First, grab a journal (or download the companion workbook from CreativeAcademyForWriters.

com/resources) and work through the Your Turn exercises below to get a sense of how you're currently feeling about co-authoring.

Your Turn

- Have you had co-authoring experience?
- What was most memorable about it? What was the best part? What was the biggest challenge?
- What is your motivation, your why, for considering co-writing?
- When you think about co-writing, what excites you most about the process?
- Who do you know who has co-authored a book? Reach out to them and ask about their experience—the good, the bad, the ugly.

2

WHAT ARE THE UPSIDES OF CO-AUTHORING?

There are lots of reasons co-authoring makes creative and business sense. As you journey through this section, keep in mind that each individual—and each collaborative partnership—has its own personality. What one person sees as an advantage, someone else might see as a disadvantage.

You can get more written in less time

Let's list this one right at the top. If you share the writing of a novel or book, you won't have to write as many words as you would writing alone.

You know the days when you're parked in front of your screen and your muse has pulled a no-show? Now imagine that, instead of dwelling on your anemic word count at the end of the day, your manuscript is actually longer despite your creative constipation, because your partner has been writing like the wind. *Bonus!*

Co-writing *can* reduce the amount of time that you need to invest in completing a project. If you want to write several projects in a time-limited period, co-authoring can help you hit *publish* more quickly.

You can share writing and publishing responsibilities

Remember the days when you imagined being a writer meant spending all your time writing? Cue knowing laughter. As any career author knows, writing is only a small portion of how you actually spend your time. You also need to handle marketing, promotion, reader engagement and your social media presence. And, if you're choosing to indie publish, yours tasks include all the elements of formatting, cover design and uploading manuscripts.

Co-writing allows you to divide and conquer all the jobs of being a working author. If you choose your co-author wisely, you may be able to focus on the specific tasks you prefer, while your partner tackles the jobs you either don't enjoy or don't do well.

Co-writing reduces the number of things on your personal to-do list.

You have a partner to help weather the storms

Writing is supposed to be fun—maybe not every day or every moment of every project, but we're distrustful of the idea that all artists are tortured souls and that writing is meant to be like bleeding on the page.

As authors, we love words and sentences and paragraphs. We love that moment when ideas fall into place and we truly understand a character's motivation or our story's direction—when the pieces of the plot come together and we can feel a happy ending on the horizon. But not every writing day is like skipping through fields of wildflowers. Some days it's more like slogging through hip-deep, foul-smelling mud.

A partner can make those difficult days more manageable and remind you that this too shall pass. And two (or many) brains are often better than one for figuring out how to get out of that mud field.

You can break through blocks more quickly

Eileen can recall meeting up with a writer friend for lunch. Wine was likely involved. During the meal, Eileen talked through the book she was working on. She'd been stuck for weeks after writing her character into a corner, and now she had no idea how to fix the situation. Eileen had tried everything, and nothing worked. She was ready to admit defeat because the book was fatally flawed.

The other writer took a sip of wine, cocked her head and said, "Have you thought about trying this?" Then she laid out the perfect solution like it was no big deal. She did it in between bites of her salad without breaking a sweat or even a crouton. It was the solution that had eluded Eileen for all that time.

What can we learn from this? Is it that Eileen is sorely lacking in imagination? No, although that is how it felt to her in the moment. Is salad a magical food that spawns creativity? No, although you should eat your veggies. It's that two heads are better than one. We think in different ways. We see things from different perspectives. We build on one another's ideas.

You may also be writing a book where a certain type of expertise is useful. If two authors were writing a thriller, and one was a lawyer and another a former police officer, they'd have a real-life *Law & Order* situation. And we all know how well that show did!

You can give plots and characters greater depth

We talked above about how different perspectives can help with brainstorming, but it's more than that—different perspectives can expand your plot and the breadth of your character's viewpoint.

When Donna was writing a romance novel with a male co-author, they would send editing notes back and forth with questions like, "Men really think that way?" and "What?! Women don't like that?"

If you've always lived in a large city but you're writing about a character who owned horses as a youth, a co-writer who's lived on a ranch will add far more depth to those equine scenes than any Internet research could provide.

If you're in your fifties, writing about a character in her early twenties, a Gen-Z co-author will add legitimacy to your story because they will intuitively know it is not cool to use the word "cool." Different life experiences show up on co-written pages in ways you might not have even considered.

Co-writing provides an opportunity for writers from different backgrounds, cultures, religions, and life experiences to expand the depth of their combined story.

You can leverage your strengths

Working with a co-author can help you leverage the benefits of different approaches to writing. For instance, on the plotter-versus-discovery-writer (a.k.a. pantster) spectrum, every writer has an approach that works best for them—and that can bring with it certain challenges. The outliner who loses interest in their story before it's finished. The pantser who writes themselves into a dead end. When the spontaneous writing approach a discovery writer brings to a project is matched with the thinking ahead that a plotter does, the benefits of both storytelling approaches are at play.

You might excel at dialogue or character development but struggle with tension and conflict. Working with a co-author who bolsters the areas where your writing needs attention can produce a stronger book.

Eileen and Crystal were both interested in writing a book about building a career as a writer. Over a dinner, they started discussing what should be included in that type of book. Eileen had information about traditional publishing, Crystal about indie. Eileen was all about the feelings, and Crystal had the skill to make an actual business plan. Together, they created a book they were both super proud of, and one that could help a much larger range of readers. (If that sounds like something you'd find helpful, check out *Full Time Author: How to Build, Grow and Maintain a Successful Writing Career that You Love* by Eileen Cook and Crystal Hunt).

Knowing and communicating your own strengths and weaknesses will allow you to search out a co-writer who will complement you and make your writing stronger. If you're not sure of your strengths, you can speak to your critique group or complete the Writer's Self-Evaluation available at CreativeAcademyForWriters.com/resources.

You benefit from a built-in accountability partner

Social scientists have researched and proven that when we're accountable to other people, we have more success reaching our goals. This is why personal trainers encourage us to have a gym buddy—you may not want to drag yourself out from under those cozy flannel sheets on a cold morning, but if someone is waiting to run laps with you, you're more likely to do it.

Accountability with writing is the same, even if you're not co-authoring. Since the inception of The Creative Academy for Writers, we've hosted twice-weekly Motivation and Accountability Mastermind groups. During these hours, members have their progress acknowledged, troubleshoot challenges, and then speak aloud their intentions for the week to come. Dozens of members credit this accountability group for directly contributing to their author success.

In terms of co-author accountability, you and your writing partner will agree on deadlines and output expectations for your shared project. Having a co-writer who is relying on you to complete your pages so they can contribute their part is one motivation to get your butt in the seat and your hands on the keyboard. Having a co-writer can drive you forward with your goals.

Donna says accountability, Eileen says peer pressure—but the productive kind, unlike the peer pressure that resulted in her asymmetrical Flock of Seagulls hairdo in the late 80s.

You can build confidence

For an early-stage writer, it can be hard to maintain perspective about what's good in our writing, our story, our plot and characters. A co-author who acknowledges your good work as you co-create a story or book can be invaluable to confidence-building.

You can shorten your learning curve in a new-to-you genre

Let's assume you've got a strong handle on what it takes to write a killer suspense novel. Now you'd like to try your hand at writing romantic suspense... but you don't read romance. Co-writing with an author familiar with the genre could save you the embarrassment (and bad reviews) that might follow if you miss the mark with reader expectations.

Also, assuming both co-authors have a following in their own genre areas, having both your names on a title can help you break into that new reader market.

And the benefits aren't just for the newbies. A writer who is more experienced in a particular genre will benefit from their co-author's perspective and story ideas, which can shake up character or plot devices that may be in need of a refresh.

You can benefit from shared promotions and audiences

Any experienced author will tell you that writing books is just one of many steps to become an earning author. Getting your book into readers' hands is a whole job unto itself. Co-writing often requires sharing promotion duties, which helps the book reach a wider audience.

A fan of your co-writer who reads and enjoys your co-written book will be more inclined to try your other titles.

This is one strong reason why authors love to write in shared worlds. Vi Keeland and Penelope Ward created a blockbuster *New York Times*–bestselling series of books called the Cocky Hero Club. There are about 200 titles in this shared-world series, penned by close to 200 authors. Why? Because the shared promotion and audience of these books has value and sales power.

Another way to share the audience of an established author brand follows the model of James Patterson and Clive Cussler. Partnering with an established author can provide you with greater visibility and a chance to grow your own career more quickly.

Both Patterson and Cussler established successful careers by writing a particular type of book, but the demand for their stories was higher than their ability to produce them. Both authors now co-write books—they generate the story idea and outline, and a co-writer writes the manuscript. The big-name author then steps back in and makes certain the final manuscript fits with their brand.

Each book is published with Patterson's or Cussler's name in a large font on the cover and the co-writer's name in a smaller font.

This type of partnership provides the new writer with a chance to reach far more readers than they would have been able to on their own.

Your published output can increase

Although we 100% believe that authors should be publishing their best possible work, it's also true that in order to earn any kind of living as an author, the number of books we have available for readers is important.

Our goal as authors is to write enough books that when readers falls in love with one of our titles, they can go back, read our entire back catalogue and eagerly count down the weeks or months to our next release. The more frequently you can meet your readers' desire for another book, the more you will cement your name in their mind.

Since co-writing typically involves a division of work, it can allow you to produce more quality books more quickly than you could on your own. More books lead to more sales. More sales lead to more energy to write more books. It's a happy circle.

Your Turn

If you have a co-author in mind, schedule some focused time with that person to discuss the upsides raised in this chapter. If you don't have a co-author in mind, use the following questions to consider your boundaries, strengths and weaknesses.

- Download and complete the Writer's Self-Evaluation to identify both your strengths and the areas where you could use author support.
- If you have a co-writer in mind, have them do the same.

- What upsides of co-authoring feel most appealing or important to you?
- Is there a benefit of co-writing that's important to you but not listed in this chapter?
- Journal using the prompt "The one thing I most hope to gain from a co-writing experience is…"

3

WHAT ARE THE CHALLENGES OF CO-AUTHORING?

You had to know it wasn't going to be *all* fun and games. In addition to the benefits of being in a co-author relationship, there are also challenges. It's important to consider these possible cons so you can decide which, if any, are co-author deal breakers for you. It'll also allow you to consider how to problem-solve around these situations if they arise.

You may not have decision-making power

How much easier would the world be if everyone we interacted with just did what we wanted them to? Alas, in a co-writing situation you may have to compromise on decisions or, in some cases, give control to the other writer. You may say that any decisions on a project are going to be split 50-50, but what is your plan if you and your partner disagree about something?

Your co-writer may have strong feelings on a pen name, the branding for the series, how the website reads, content for ads, or sales of subsidiary rights—from audiobooks to the choice to accept an option for film. You may not be in a position to counter these decisions if the other writer has taken the "lead" on a project. If the two of you haven't discussed how to handle these types of disagreements, you may find yourself stuck and unable to move forward.

You may disagree on creative directions

We made the choice to place creative directions in its very own category. One of the joys of writing is the opportunity to create a world and characters. If you want the character to have the magical ability to transform anything they want into chocolate, then they can have that skill. (Give us a call if you work this out in real life.) However, when co-writing, you need to share those creative decisions, from character descriptions and motivations to plot points and what constitutes your character's dark moment of the soul.

A writer who isn't fussed about which font to use on a co-author website may feel much differently about the actions a character would make in a particular situation. As writers we become very attached to our imaginary friends, and co-writing means sharing a vision of those people who exist in our minds.

If you're writing non-fiction, you may think this is less relevant, but it still holds true. Co-writing a project will mean agreeing on key points and how you want to have information communicated. Decisions on what to include in your book and what to ignore can take on new importance if you and your co-author have different views or experiences with the subject matter.

You must share rules in an established world

In the section What Kind of Co-author Relationship Is Right for You? we'll discuss the different forms that co-writing can take. In several of these models, co-authorship is not about writing one book together—it's about writing within an established world or author brand. In those situations, you have to agree to work within boundaries set by the world owner. In some cases, these can be quite strict. Knowing all the rules of writing in an established world is critical research to do *before* signing any co-author contract. (Contract? Yup. We'll talk about those later).

The most critical challenge to be aware of when you consider joining a shared-universe book series is if you'll be required to include specific characters or plot lines—even if they feel extraneous—in the story you want to tell.

You share voice and tone

Ah, author voice. Few topics are as much fun to drop into conversation with a group of writers. Every author we know has received at least one letter from an agent or publisher who passed on their manuscript because they "didn't connect with the voice."

In theory, author voice is easy to define—it refers to style, what makes a writer's words sound uniquely like *them*. But to go a level deeper and identify the specifics of a certain author's voice is more difficult. Defining author voice has been compared to defining obscenity: it's hard to describe, but you know it when you see it—or, in this case, read it.

With more than one writer on a project, those different voices must blend into one so seamlessly that readers won't be able to tell which of the co-authors contributed a specific paragraph, scene or chapter. You need the story as whole to flow as one piece, with a consistent writing style and story tone and a seamless balance of narration, description, dialogue, and all the other storytelling building blocks.

The challenge is greatest when co-authors each have their own distinctive voices. This isn't to say a joint project won't work, but it will require one or all of the co-authors to adapt their natural voice so all voices blend and appear consistent to readers. Or, you can structure your co-writing in a way that preserves those voices and uses them for different characters.

You share timelines and deadlines

The benefit of a shared timeline is motivation to stay on track and finish your writing project more quickly than you would on your own. The downside is that if one co-author misses a deadline, the ripple effect can wreak havoc on other projects, on family time, and on stress levels.

Most co-authors we know are also writing books on their own. Those other books have deadlines too—with beta readers, editors and online distributers. Sometimes adjusting these deadlines is easy. Other times, having one project fall behind can create a perfect storm for either burnout or project failure—which, of course, creates a new set of challenges to deal with the work that's already been co-written.

You might disagree on the division and quality of work

Almost everyone has a story from their school days of being involved in a group project from hell. There was always *someone* in the group who either didn't do their part or "called it in" with a half-assed job.

In a co-author relationship, the project will be presented to a broader audience than just your high school teacher, so it's critical for the partners to have a shared understanding of what constitutes "good enough" in the co-authored book.

If expectations aren't well aligned, it can leave one party feeling that they have to take on more work than they'd expected to bring the project up to their standard.

There will be conflict

All relationships—even the healthiest ones—experience conflict at some point. Personality differences, honest miscommunication, and all the challenges we've listed above can trigger a dark moment of the co-author's soul, when it feels like all is lost and the mountain to completing the joint project is just too high to climb.

We hate to say it, but the odds are ever in your favour that you will experience conflict when you co-write. The trick isn't to avoid it, but to be prepared to deal with it in a mature and respectful way. We discuss this in the section How Do You Resolve Conflicts in the Writing Process?

Business complications

As an author, you are running a business. You have expenses. Hopefully, you offset some of those costs with royalties. You run your individual author business in a certain way.

But make no mistake—co-authoring is a business relationship. And business relationships bring the necessary challenge of paperwork and contracts.

Here are a few of the many questions you and your co-author will need to discuss and agree on.

- Will you seek agent representation for your shared work?
- How will royalties be tracked and divided?
- Who will prepare tax documents?
- Will you incorporate your co-author business?
- If you're co-authoring a series, what happens if one of you wants to stop?

Problems arise in co-author partnerships if these questions, and many more, aren't considered *before* something goes wrong—or very right! We tend to go into situations expecting best-case scenarios, which is wonderful, but both success and challenges can cause complications.

When we originally set out to write The Creative Academy Guides for Writers, it was a bright idea that came out of a bout of day-drinking at a conference. We'd been working together for two years, building The Creative Academy. We liked each other. We liked working together. We had huge respect for our different knowledge bases. It seemed like a no-brainer to write books together!

It wasn't until we began working on the books in this series that we understood the depth and breadth of complications that can arise from co-writing. Complications aren't bad things, but we do need to plan for them. One way we did that was by playing a game we called "What is the worst thing that could happen?"

There are many benefits of working with others, not the least being that it's a lot of fun! But from a business perspective, it's *easier* to write books on your own. The paperwork, tracking and systems increase when you partner with one or more creators. Many of these complications only become clear as you go through the process. We highlight several of these in this book so you can avoid or plan around common business complications to co-authoring.

Your Turn

If you have a co-author in mind, schedule some focused time with that person to discuss the challenges raised in this chapter. If you don't have a co-author in mind, consider your boundaries, strengths and weaknesses with the following questions.

- If you haven't already done so, download and complete

the Writer's Self-Evaluation to identify your strengths and areas where you could use author support.
- If you have a co-writer in mind, have them do the same.
- What challenges of co-authoring concern or excite you?
- Is there a downside to co-writing that concerns you but is not listed in this chapter?
- Journal using the prompt "The one thing I most hope to avoid in a co-writing experience is…"

PART II

HOW CAN YOU COLLABORATE WITH OTHER AUTHORS?

4

WHAT KIND OF CO-AUTHOR RELATIONSHIP IS RIGHT FOR YOU?

Many kinds of writing can be shared with a co-author—novels, short stories, non-fiction books, blogs, courses, academic papers, screenplays, recipes, magazine articles, podcast scripts… The list is long and as creative as the people who have ideas to share with words.

Presumably, since you're reading this book, you have at least a broad idea about what you and your future co-author could be writing together.

Although most of the examples we cite in this book come from fiction co-authors, the three of us have first-hand experience as co-authors of non-fiction (as evidenced by the words you're reading now). In most situations, however, whether you're co-authoring a play meant for Broadway or a book to help Broadway actors find their inner Alexander Hamilton or Angelica Schuyler, the guidance is the same. Where things might be different, we'll make that clear.

In the sections that follow, we share tips and things to watch for in a variety of co-author models. But one relationship we don't address in its own section is one the three of us, and many of members of The Creative Academy for Writers, engage in: co-authoring *lite*.

It would be an oversight not to mention the kind of co-author help that many, many writers get from, and give to, their trusted peers: editing and bringing ideas to the table at different stages of a book's development. Like the friend who effortlessly pulled Eileen out of a corner she'd written herself into, peer advisors provide ideas that can be crucial to plot and character development. Without these trusted colleagues' input, our stories would not be nearly as good.

Did you know that J. R. R. Tolkien and C. S. Lewis revised each other's manuscripts yet never credited each other on their books?

Even though those friends were not actual co-authors, we mention their relationship because it had the qualities you should look for in a more invested co-author relationship.

So if you've drawn on another author's guidance and support for a book you've written before, you already have a sense of a strong co-author relationship. It's one where the other person hears you, gets you, understands your stories, loves your characters, and wants to see you succeed, while you feel the same about them and their stories.

Our co-author relationships

Crystal, Eileen and Donna are co-authors on three levels.

- We are all individual authors in a series called The Creative Academy Guides for Writers. It's our shared non-fiction world.
- We are all informal collaborators (editors) on several books in the series that have just one of our names on the cover.

- We are all fully credited co-authors on books in the series that have two or three of our names on the cover.

Before writing books in this series, all three of us were published authors with long writing careers. We'd all checked our writing egos at the door years earlier. Eileen had written 15 books for traditional publishers; Crystal had written and co-written numerous children's books and non-fiction books and indie-published several romance novellas; and Donna, in addition to having indie published one novel and co-authored one non-fiction book, had 20 years of non-fiction ghostwriting experience written in invisible ink on her resume.

We all understood the necessity of keeping emotion out of the writing equation. We also intimately knew each other's author strengths and weaknesses because we'd worked together for two years, launching and running a start-up business—The Creative Academy for Writers.

When we first conceived of the Creative Academy Guides for Writers series, we knew from that initial meeting that we'd be writing books individually and together. From day one, the three of us wanted to be co-authors in all the ways.

Collectively, we made a list of over 20 topics we wanted to write about. Some of them, like *Full Time Author*, lent themselves well to a co-author approach. Others, like *Strategic Series Author*, covered a subject that, at the time of writing, only Crystal had experience with, so it made sense for her to write it on her own. Eileen and Donna were her highly engaged developmental editors.

Eileen's experience and expertise writing traditionally published novels and teaching fiction courses made her the perfect person in our co-author team to write *Build Better Characters* and *Create Story Conflict*—titles with just her name on the cover.

What readers can't see is that, behind the scenes, the co-author relationships and agreements on those two books are very different. One book distributes royalties and marketing expenses equally among the three of us as co-authors; the other does not. One book cost Eileen out-of-pocket for editing and ongoing ad management expenses; the other did not. The splits were a business decision we made based on our goals for The Creative Academy for Writers.

This is the level of thinking you need to do right now, before you've started to write with a co-author. Because once you're in the mud, it's a little late to be deciding who's responsible for the jobs and expenses related to getting that great book idea onto shelves.

In a later section, we address the specifics of the business side of co-authoring, but keep that business relationship in mind as you consider what co-author model will suit you best.

Your Turn

Are you new to co-writing?

- Do you have a particular model of co-writing in mind already? Describe that relationship in as much detail as you can imagine, from how often you'll talk with your co-author while you're writing your manuscript to who will handle social media posts and write engagement emails.
- Reflect on the "co-writing lite" relationships you've had.
- What was most valuable to you and your manuscript?
- What parts of the interaction did you enjoy most?
- What parts were most challenging?

If you've co-written before—even if you didn't complete a manuscript or publish it—think about that relationship.

- How did you define the relationship and divide tasks?
- What parts of that process worked well for you?
- What parts would you prefer not to repeat in a new co-author experience?

5
TWO OR MORE WRITERS WRITING UNDER ONE PEN NAME

If you play trivia games, here's a question you can toss into the mix to win yourself points: Which author on this list is actually two people writing under one name?

- Ellery Queen (crime fiction)
- Michael Gregario (historical crime fiction)
- Nicci French (psychological thrillers)
- Max Monroe (contemporary romance)
- Christina Lauren (contemporary romance)
- Melanie Shawn (contemporary romance)

And the answer… They are *all* co-author duos!

The decision to choose a single pen name to brand your co-author relationship or put both your names on the cover may not seem important at first. But as an author, your name is your brand, so what you publish under that name is very important to your author business.

Here are a few reasons a pair—or group—of writers might decide to use a single pen name instead of their real names.

One or both authors have an established following

Sometimes, an established author with a readership in one genre doesn't want to confuse those readers by publishing books in other genres. Even a subgenre change can be detrimental to an author who has one-click-buy readers.

We've heard first-hand stories from romance-writing friends who made the mistake of changing the steam level in their books and upsetting readers. And how do readers who don't get what they expect express their displeasure? They leave lousy reviews.

This was why Crystal chose to write under multiple pen names: CJ Hunt for her contemporary romances, Jean Hunt for her cozy mysteries, Crystal Hunt for non-fiction and Crystal Stranaghan for her children's books. Readers in those genres all have distinct preferences.

Most authors who've been around the publishing block a couple of times know the risks of messing with their author brand. So, if you're looking to build a co-author relationship with an established author, they may insist on a single-name pseudonym.

There are contract obligations with a publisher or agent

If one or both of you have been traditionally published, your agent might prefer that your experimental new side hustle not risk the brand you've been building in the traditional publishing world.

If you have a publishing contract with an option clause—where your publisher gets first crack at your next work—it's critical to know if it allows you to publish a co-authored project under a pseudonym. Option clauses vary widely. Some claim first rights to any next work you produce, while some are very narrow, claiming rights for something as specific as the next novel-length YA fantasy you write.

Your publisher may have concerns that any new book you write will "poach" readers who would have bought the book you did with them. In this case they might prefer that you use a pen name.

The most important thing is to be transparent with your publisher and agent, and to ensure that you know all of your contractual agreements so you're not in violation. Remember, your agent is your business representative. They need to know what you're doing so they can best help direct your career.

One or both authors want to hide their real identity

For the same reasons some authors like to keep their personal and professional lives separate (the obvious—an elementary school teacher who publishes gruesome stories about serial killers), co-authors may find it in their best interest to build an author persona that is not directly connected to either their real lives or to their individual author personas.

When Donna and a man we'll call Tony (because that's his name!) had coffee at a conference a couple of years ago and decided to take a stab at this whole co-author thing, Tony had a thriller on contract with a publisher and Donna had a humour novel published. Their desired co-author genre was a far cry from both thriller and humour, so they thought it would be most strategic to co-author under a pen name. But they waffled, with ego being a thing and both wanting to build their author street creds even if it meant writing in wildly different genres.

But when the character they were writing together made her penchant for public acts of nudity known, they made the firm decision to write under a pen name. Why? They didn't want their young adult children to be traumatized by reading the steamy scenes from Mom and Dad's imaginations. Neither Donna nor Tony had the budget to pay for that amount of counselling for their kids.

It makes strategic sense

At least historically speaking, some readers, either consciously or unconsciously, choose stories written by authors of one gender more than another, especially in particular genres. While we fully support a world in which good stories are just good stories —regardless of the author's gender—the unfortunate reality is that we're not quite there yet as a society.

Romance readers, predominantly women, show a preference for stories written by women, for instance.

Readers of science fiction and thrillers give male authors more of a chance than female authors.

Though not a co-author situation, J. K. Rowling was advised by her publisher to use initials when the first Harry Potter book was published, to hide the fact that the author was a woman. When she chose to write adult mysteries, she went with the name Robert Galbraith.

Although we didn't speak directly to the mixed-gender co-author teams behind Nicci French or Michael Gregario, we assume there was a strategy behind their choice of co-author pseudonyms.

You don't want to confuse the algorithms

Sometimes adding a single initial or changing a spelling very slightly is enough to ensure that the algorithms driving the online bookstores don't get confused about what kind of books to associate with a specific author name. There are powerful AI engines driving what Amazon and other stores show you when you go online shopping. They're set up to make educated guesses about what you are most likely to purchase next based on your browsing and buying history.

If you'd like to learn more about this, we highly recommend reading David Gaughran's books *Let's Get Digital* and *Amazon*

Decoded, which explain how all this technical wizardry works. But it's the same logic that drove Netflix to allow different family members to set up their own profiles. That way your watch history doesn't confuse the algorithms into searching for animated romantic-comedy thrillers. While it would be entertaining to see what titles they might suggest, their chances of satisfying both the thriller lover and their rom-com-watching spouse are slim.

In the book world, if the computer can't tell who will like your book, it won't know who to recommend it to. So it will recommend it to no one. Using different author names stops those "also-bought" lists from populating with the wrong kinds of recommendations, and it keeps your readers happier with the recommendations they receive.

Your Turn

- Do you have a personal reason to keep your co-author identity separate from your real name?
- How important is it for you to be 100% anonymous? This must be clear to your co-author.
- Would it be more or less strategic to separate your co-author brand from your existing author brand and name?
- How much marketing value does your current author name bring to the table?
- Will your co-authored books cater to the interests of your existing readers?

- Will your co-authored books potentially upset existing readers?
- Do you have works under contract with a traditional publisher? If so, what have you contractually agreed to in terms of other writing?
- Do you have an agent? If so, ask them for their recommendations and concerns regarding a co-author arrangement—*before* you sign any contracts with a co-author.

6

TWO OR MORE WRITERS WRITING UNDER THEIR OWN NAMES

Even decades after the deaths of Bud Abbott and Lou Costello, this film-writing duo, who co-wrote and acted in more than 40 films together, is still known.

Mick Jagger and Keith Richards, the songwriting team behind the Rolling Stones, wrote more than 300 songs with each other.

Avis Lang was Neil deGrasse Tyson's editor for years before they made the leap to co-author a book.

Wouldn't it be great to go back to your high school reunion and stand on the stage in your old auditorium, accepting loving applause and admiration for being one of the names in a famous writing duo? Yeah. Yeah, it would!

As much as we tell you to leave your ego at the door when you work with a co-author, no one says you can't embrace that ego when you're basking in the glory of being a household name.

Barker, Hunt and Cook… Has a nice ring to it, doesn't it? Though it does sound more like the name of a caveman equipment store than a dynamic trio of authors who write fun, playful, and helpful guides for writers.

Although there are many reasons to make up a shared name for your co-author partnership, there are also lots of smart reasons to use your own.

One or both authors have an established following

Yes, this is the exact same reason you and your co-author may decide *not* to write as a team under your own names.

Imagine you're both mystery writers and have decided to pen a thriller together. In this situation, your shared story will have a similar tone and blood-loss quotient as your other books, so you might not worry about upsetting your existing fans.

If you already have a following, you'll have a built-in market right out of the printing press. The author duo that assumes a new and unknown name will have to build their marketing machine from scratch. You earned those Facebook, Instagram and Twitter followers. Your email list loves getting news about your new releases. They'll be the first fans of your new writing venture.

You have complementary areas of expertise

This is an especially beneficial reason for co-authors of non-fiction to use their real names. If you're co-writing a book that blends knowledge and expertise from two distinct fields, having two experts' names on the cover better than doubles the credibility of the shared project.

What do you get when a professor of economics (Steven Levitt) teams up to write with an award-winning journalist (Stephen Dubner)? In this bestselling situation, you get *Freakonomics*, a book that's sold over five million copies in 40 languages.

Although we weren't eavesdropping on the discussion that led them to co-author that first book, we would wager that writing under a shared pseudonym wasn't ever on the table. Why would it be when these two individuals had names that would not only help them in their publishing pursuits but also boost their reputations in their other jobs?

You're both just starting out and have nothing to lose

If you're brand new to publishing—and the book you're co-authoring won't earn you the side-eye from your boss or the parents at your kid's school—publishing under both your names can be a great strategy to launch a writing career.

In the same way an established author can leverage their existing followers when they co-author a book, if or when you decide to write something on your own, you'll already have readers who know your name and love your work.

That said, there's no law that says the name you use in your co-author relationship has to be the name your friends and family know you by. You could use a pseudonym that is the same or different from the one you ultimately use when you publish on your own.

You'll want to do some thinking about whether or not you envision yourself writing in multiple genres down the line, or if a career change is looming on the horizon.

Your Turn

- Do you or your co-author have an established following you want to leverage?
- Will your author brand benefit from having more titles published in your own name? How will this be beneficial?

- Is your track record, knowledge, publishing history or expertise relevant to the book you're co-writing? What specific value does your name bring?

7

HEADLINER AND CO-AUTHOR

If you're a fan of Clive Cussler, James Patterson or Tom Clancy, you'll be familiar with this form of co-authorship relationship—at least the way it appears on the cover of a book, if not how it plays out on the pages inside.

One of the truths about being a career author is that in order to earn enough money to pay a mortgage and drink the high-end brands of your favourite beverage, you have to publish a lot of books. It's the rare author who has one or two giant hits that support them for rest of their working lives. Most need to have a constant stream of content coming out into the market. It's simple math, really. The more books you have available for a reader once they finish reading a story they love, the more money you'll make.

Think about the authors you impatiently await new releases from. For Donna, it's mystery and police procedural author Louise Penny. For Eileen, it's thriller author Robyn Harding. And Crystal is first in virtual line to pre-order new titles from Nora Roberts or J. D. Robb.

Each of these authors (or pen names, in the case of Nora Roberts and J. D. Robb) publishes, on average, one or two books a year. Imagine how many more books they'd sell to their super fans if they were to publish three, four or even five books a year of the same quality. At the very least, they could double their royalties.

Enter the co-author relationships in which a million-copy-selling author teams up with a lesser-known writer to increase output. In addition to the guys who've used this approach for dozens of titles, a solid handful of other successful writers, like Janet Evanovich, Mary Higgins Clark, Bella Andre and Skye Warren, have embraced this form of co-authorship to meet the unrelenting demand for new books from their voracious readers.

What does this co-author relationship look like?

Of course, we haven't seen the contracts of any these authors, but a handful have spoken about their process, and there are consistencies in their stories.

These well-known authors have a popular series of books that share many things in common, like a main character, a particular type of secondary character, and a storyline that contains certain beats. Readers have expectations about the tone, the way their stories roll out, and the level of action, heat, blood loss or magic (depending on the genre). One could say that books in these co-authored series follow a bit of a formula.

These big-name authors (BNAs) outline the major plot points and beats, characters and stakes, and locations of the story they have in mind. They give that outline to a smaller-name author (SNA).

The SNA writes a first draft of a story based on BNA's outline.

BNA reads the draft and gives feedback for revisions to SNA.

SNA makes the changes, and BNA adds the final flourishes to the story so it shines in the series world.

Editors, publishers and book distributors do their thing, and then readers run to their favourite book retailer to pick up the new story.

Readers are happy, and big- and small-name authors count the money that rolls in.

Sounds like a dream co-author partnership. And, for many writers who've earned the trust of a BNA, it likely is, since many series keep one co-author for the duration of the run, which can be a dozen books or more. Clive Cussler, for instance, has several popular series, each with its own co-author. What a great way to crank out six full-length novels a year.

How does one become a small-name author for a big-name author?

Unless you have your own large backlist, you probably won't land a co-author gig with a big-name author. However, if you've written and published at least a few well-received books in a genre, you may be in a good position to approach a medium-name author to work with.

The section Where Can You Find a Writing Partner? goes into detail about this, since approaching any author requires the same steps—it's just the expectation of getting a yes that changes from one prospect to the next.

Your Turn

- Do you write in the same genre as either a big- or medium-name author whose books you automatically purchase?

- Is this an author you would like to work with?
- If so, do some research about them. Do they have co-authored titles?
- Do they engage with readers on social media? If yes, start a conversation—but *not* by immediately asking them to partner with you!
- Search their website to determine if there is a submission form or an explanation of how to apply to work with them.

8

SHARED-WORLD STORIES

Co-writing relationships in which several authors write individual stories in a shared world are very popular in both the romance, science fiction and fantasy genres.

This relationship usually works one of two ways.

1. An established author has a series that is doing well. As with the big-name author situation, readers want more books in that world, more quickly than the author can release them.
2. An author has an idea for a world they think would appeal to readers, creates a world bible and invites authors to participate in the series.

In most shared-world co-author relationships, everyone is fully responsible for writing their own titles within the parameters of certain world-building expectations.

Participating in this kind of co-author partnership allows you to leverage the marketing power of every author in the series, which will, in theory at least, introduce you to new readers.

Let's explore these co-authored world scenarios in a bit more detail.

An established series seeks stories

One popular example of this first approach is the Cocky Hero Club that's based on the bestselling Cocky Bastard series by Vi Keeland and Penelope Ward. The books in the spinoff series include characters and story settings from the original six books by Keeland and Ward.

Once accepted into the Cocky Hero Club, authors have their books branded with the highly recognizable goat logo. The books are promoted on the Cocky Hero Club website. At the time of writing, more than 250 authors have been published by this imprint.

A world idea seeks authors

An emerging trend is when multiple authors come together, and each writes one (or more) books in a series. In this co-author model, each author publishes their book(s) from their own KDP account. Then, all the co-authors link their books together as a series. They do this either with support from KDP staff or by including one "author name" that is actually the series name. This decoy author name is then used to set up the series page. This allows authors to collaboratively promote their titles, to encourage read-through by readers, and to release a series much more quickly than they could if one author were responsible for writing all the books.

This co-author model is so popular that some Facebook groups exist just to connect authors who want to collaborate in this way.

Donna found a shared world that appealed to her in one of these groups. Author Rebecca Norinne had created a fictitious New England college and town for two full-length novels and three novellas. She'd done a great deal of world-building for those titles and decided to make use of that work by inviting other authors to write stories centred around students attending Thackeray College.

It may not be the case with all shared-world collections, but, in this one, Donna is pleased to have developed relationships with a dozen other authors who are at her author business level—some of whom she plans to work and grow her readership with.

Things to consider before writing in a shared world

As nice an ego boost as it would be to write in a world that's part of a bestselling series, it's important to know, like with all your author decisions, what business goal you hope to achieve from the association.

- Is it an ego boost to have your name sit on the same shelf as an A-list author?
- Are you a huge fan of the world and feel a deep desire to write in it?
- Do you want to develop relationships with other authors in the series?
- Are you hoping to earn significant royalties from the association?

You should ask and get answers to these questions (and many more) before you sign a contract to write in a shared world—because you will be forfeiting certain rights in exchange for the benefits of being connected to another author's world. It's important to know whether those benefits match your goals.

For instance, if your goal is to earn a living as an indie author, pay attention to the way royalties for your titles will be split, who owns audio rights, who owns foreign language rights—you might be surprised at how many European countries want translations of American fiction—and the terms of getting your rights back if the book is not selling under the series-world imprint.

In the shared world Donna joined, there was a buy-in amount that paid for project management and cover designs for all of the titles in the series. All authors had to commit to putting their title in Kindle Unlimited and pricing it at $0.99 until the last of the 12 books had completed their KU contract—which meant that Donna's title, released on the first day of the series, would be locked in at $0.99 for two 90-day periods. That means she makes $0.30 for each sale. For people who read the book using the Kindle Unlimited account, Donna earns around just $0.50. This is not a get-rich-quick book, despite the shared marketing and promotions from the other authors.

And that's okay with her because Donna's goals heading into this co-author relationship were (a) to write and publish a novella, something she'd wanted to try but needed accountability to actually commit to; and (b) to collaborate with other authors for a relatively short term, to test the waters and see if she liked working within shared-world constraints.

Some of the constraints she loved, such as writing in a pre-built world and working with other authors to arrange character cameos between books. The length constraint, however, was an unwelcome challenge since her story was limited to 20,000 words when it *really* wanted another 3,000.

Overall, it was an excellent experience. Donna now knows that the next shared world she joins as a co-author will have to give her the flexibility to write a longer story.

Case Study: Mia Harlan

Mia Harlan is a twice-awarded *USA Today* Bestselling Author whose main shared-world experience was founding and running, along with Eva Delaney, a series of paranormal, reverse-harem, multi-author books set in a town called Silver

Springs. She has co-authored over half a dozen titles both in and outside this shared world.

Mia's co-authoring adventure started when she was in middle school. She and her best friend were writing a book together when her friend's family moved away. They continued to co-write by email and in 2014 published their story on Smashwords. She said that co-writing this book kept her friendship going with a friend she couldn't see in person anymore.

Many years later, in her job as a librarian, Mia ran a writers group for seniors. The members of the group wanted to publish the stories they'd written, so Mia made that happen. The co-authors in the anthology published paperback copies and held book signings on a not-for-profit basis. The project was so successful she organized a second anthology for members of the library's writers group. She also helped another library create a similar program—to which Mia contributed a story.

Mia is a connector. She loves engaging with other writers and with readers. She's also a visionary who is not afraid to ask for help or assign tasks to teammates. And, based on the number of people who have written in more than one series in the shared world Mia and Eva created, authors appreciate her co-author approach to publishing. Based on sales, it's also working for readers.

So what does that model look like?

Mia and author friend Eva Delaney looked around for a successful co-authored series on which to model their own. They analyzed the branding, marketing, and release schedule for books in the series. They took that information and conceived and planned a series in a genre they believed would be popular: reverse-harem paranormal romance.

And the town of Silver Springs was founded.

They created a recruitment brochure with details about their town and elements that would have to be included in every title in the series. At the core of the town is a little shop called Jewels Cafe, which sells a pumpkin-spice latte that helps people recognize their fated mates.

Twelve authors joined the Jewels Cafe series. All contributors shared publishing and marketing tasks, from cover design to social media graphics to handling the many details about the town. The management of the world takes about 30 hours a week between all the necessary tasks and conversations at all stages, from plot conception through writing, publishing and marketing.

The experience of the first series was so much fun—the key indicator Mia uses to when choosing where to focus her time—that 6 of the 12 co-authors joined forces to write a second series (Mia refers to them as "seasons"). The second series focused on the town library and a book that's been enchanted so that, when read, it allows the heroine to find her fated mate. Six new authors joined the series, bringing the total of original titles to 12.

Evidence of the success of this shared world is the number of authors who have written follow-up books in their series.

Mia and Eva also guided a group of Silver Springs superfans-turned-authors to create a sister town called Moonlit Falls for authors who want to write in the universe but don't have a home in Silver Springs. The Moonlit Falls series uses a modified version of the Silver Springs branding and even has its own pumpkin-spice latte!

This world is not managed by Mia, though the Silver Springs team oversees it. The Moonlit Falls co-authors sign a contract to meet the universe rules and standards. They receive training in marketing and publishing, and get to use the Silver Springs resources like its social media and newsletter list.

Two key factors have helped make the Silver Springs shared universe a success. First, its authors write good stories in a genre readers want to read. Second, every co-author actively markets not just their title but all the releases and titles in each season.

Mia has learned that there are two kinds of people who join a shared world.

1. Authors who want to work as part of a team to achieve a goal. They want to develop relationships that will last for several books and many years.
2. Authors who want the benefit of group marketing but don't want to support their co-authors' success or play for the long term.

You can guess which ones become family in Silver Springs.

Your Turn

- If you're interested in learning which shared-world series are looking for co-authors, search the term *boxed set* on Facebook and join some groups.
- Make a list of the reasons you're interested in being a co-author in a shared world.
- When you find a possible fit, compare your list to the restrictions and benefits of the different worlds that are seeking co-authors in your genre.
- If you can't find a shared world that brings you joy, or you have your own ideas about a shared world you'd like to create, reach out to authors who've managed shared worlds to find out what's involved in starting and running a group.

9

GHOSTWRITING AND WRITING FOR HIRE

Writing for hire is one of the more unusual forms of co-writing, but we felt it was important to include so that you can consider all your options. While in this model you are not likely an equal "co"-writer, you are still collaboratively working with someone to create a project.

What is writing for hire?

In this model, you are hired to write a book with set parameters. You may be paid a flat fee for the project, or there may be a royalty-share scenario. This is one of the things you'll want to check out before you commit to the project. Neither option is necessarily better than the other, but you need to know which one your contract specifies and make sure you feel happy with that plan. You may be working on the project under your own name, or you may be working under a set pen name or the name of another individual.

Ghostwriting

Ghostwriting does not refer to writing from beyond the grave or tapping into your psychic abilities to help the deceased tell their story. Instead, it describes a model in which a writer is hired to write someone else's story.

We don't want to shock you, but you know those celebrity books? Sometimes they don't write them themselves. (Gasp!) A celebrity may have an idea for a novel or non-fiction book, but the actual writing part is less interesting to them. They may have an outline and a desire to weigh in during the writing process, but often another writer does the heavy creative lifting.

A business executive popular on the public speaking circuit may want a book that outlines their approaches and strategies, but they might not have the time or interest for the actual writing part.

Or someone may have already written something, perhaps a personal family story, and they need a professional to polish it and carry it over the finish line.

As a ghostwriter, you'll likely be unnamed. In fact, you may be contractually required to keep your involvement a secret.

Books for hire

Occasionally publishers or individuals have an idea for a book but seek a writer to bring the idea to life. Crystal has written many such books for an educational publisher. Eileen wrote two novels for a publisher who had an idea but needed a writer. You may or may not be credited for this type of work, and you're typically provided with an outline of what the publisher wants included. The amount of creative freedom you have will vary depending on the project.

Book packagers

There are publishers who specialize in creating series and books to fit a particular niche. This is particularly common with books that fall into the middle grade or YA category. Often these books are listed as having one author but in fact are written by a number of writers. One of the best-known packaged series is the Nancy Drew series. The books were created by the publisher Edward Stratemeyer as the match to its Hardy Boys series. Carolyn Keene was the listed author, but this was a shared pen name. In cases like this, the publisher provides a detailed series "bible" so that all the books have consistency with respect to locations, characters, plots, and so on.

A non-fiction example of a packaged series is the For Dummies series. The publisher has a well-known series of how-to guides that cover everything from software programs to photography to Shakespeare. They hire different authors for these titles depending on the subject matter.

If you're interested in ghostwriting, writing a book for hire, or working with a book packager, you'll typically need a body of work for the publisher to review to ensure you'd be a good fit for their subject or storyline. Most will also ask you to write a sample chapter or two to prove your voice works for the project.

If you work with an agent, it's important to let them know you're interested in this type of work—for their advice, their connections and their cautions.

Your Turn

- If you're interested in one of these approaches to co-writing, make a list of the benefits to your author career you expect or hope to experience.

- Make a list of what you might have to give up if you were to become a ghostwriter.
- Reach out to your writing communities and find a few people who've done this kind of work. Ask if they'd spend an hour with you, sharing their real-life experiences, tips and cautions.

10

ANTHOLOGIES AND BOXED SETS

The models we describe in this section aren't technically co-author relationships, but ink is cheap and they warrant a nod since this kind of publication credit can be a gateway to more substantive co-author agreements. Also, anthologies and boxed sets have become quite popular in recent years, so we want to share some tips about getting involved in a group project like this.

First off, let's clarify the definition of *anthology* and *boxed set*, since they're often used interchangeably.

Both are publications that contain the writing of several authors under one cover. It's generally accepted in the writing community that an anthology contains short works (poems, short stories, novellas and possibly novelettes) and that boxed sets are collections of novels pulled together and sold under one cover. While anthologies typically have multiple authors, boxed sets can have multiple authors or be a collection of novels or novellas from the same author.

Collections like these can be a lot of work to manage—so what makes them so popular? We'll look at a few of the most popular types to understand why.

Anthologies curated by a publisher

You'll no doubt have heard of the *Chicken Soup for the Soul* series of anthologies. In this case, the publisher decides on a theme for the anthology and makes a call for submissions that range from short stories to longer works.

One of the key benefits of publishing a piece of writing in a curated anthology is credibility, especially if your author goals include finding an agent. Like prestigious writing awards, publications that have gold-stamped your work can help raise your submission above the noise.

In many cases, contributing authors are also paid for their story —from as little as ten dollars to hundreds of dollars—and are given paperback copies of the title in which their work appears.

There are anthology publishers who charge authors to participate in their publications. But it's important to be aware that those titles, while legitimate books, may not carry the same professional weight as book brands that are commonly seen in brick-and-mortar bookstores.

Anthologies designed to hit a list

Another common reason to be a co-author in an anthology is to "get your letters"—that is, to earn the right to call yourself a bestselling author by publishing in a volume that lands on the *USA Today, New York Times* or *Wall Street Journal* bestseller lists.

Waving an "Amazon bestseller" flag is no longer a very prestigious claim since so many authors assume the title simply for hitting the number-one spot in a sub-sub-sub-sub-subgenre on the day their book was being promoted for free. Using this metric, authors who have sold as few as six copies have claimed Amazon bestseller status, which is becoming less valuable as a marker of legitimacy.

But hitting one of the big-three bestseller lists *does* require selling—for actual dollars from people's bank accounts—many thousands of copies of a title in a limited time period. (Note that these three lists count sales only to US buyers. So if you're a non-American author with a large following in your own country, purchases from your home country's readers, while lovely, will not help you or your anthology teammates hit one of the coveted lists.)

Hundreds, if not thousands, of indie authors, especially in the romance genre, have joined forces in recent years to earn their *USA Today* Bestselling Author titles. And the easiest way for a newer writer to achieve this is by joining a co-authored anthology.

Is it an ego stroke? Sure it is!

But more than that, "having your letters" can build author credibility in a highly saturated market that sees thousands of books being published every week, all of them competing for readers. Many authors believe that being a *USA Today*, *New York Times*, or *Wall Street Journal* bestselling author increases the chance that their books will be accepted for coveted BookBub Feature deals.

Another benefit of participating in an anthology that earns you bestselling-author status is the relationships you can develop with other authors who have earned that title.

One way authors raise the visibility of new releases is by providing editorial reviews for each other. When a review is from a bestselling author, it may nudge a potential reader to try you out.

Things to consider when looking for an anthology or boxed set to join

Not all collections set the goal of becoming bestsellers as their primary target, and that is the very first thing to know when you're looking for a set to join.

Anthologies designed with the primary purpose to hit a list will always require a financial buy-in. This money will be used to compensate the person organizing the set and pay for cover design and sometimes ads. Buy-in amounts vary greatly. At the low end you can expect to pay US$200, and at the high end up to $5,000. The exception is any anothology or boxed set curated by a traditional publisher which will not ask for any funds from the authors.

Does a higher buy-in guarantee earning those letters? Nope! Here's a story from author Kat Parrish on her first (failed) attempt to hit a bestseller list.

> My partner was in a boxed set that listed at *USA Today*, so he got his letters. And yes, I'm competitive. So I specifically started looking for boxed sets that were interested in listing. The first one I signed up with cost half-a-thousand dollars (which I say that way since it sounds like more than $500).
>
> But from the start it seemed to be a doomed venture since most of us were newbies. We did not have the mailing lists. And I believe all of us were brand new to the whole ordeal that is list-aiming, so we made a lot of mistakes. That was a sobering experience.
>
> My first tip is to make sure the anthology or boxed set has at least one heavy-hitter to anchor the set. Also, look for a supportive leader, someone who's successfully managed a run for a list and who has ideas that are not the same old same old, because those old ideas aren't enough.

Here's why Mia Harlan loves anthologies, in her words.

> I've joined several anthologies to get my *USA Today* bestseller letters for my pen names.
>
> When I first started out, I ran two newsletter-builder anthologies to build email subscriber lists for myself and author friends in my genre.
>
> I join charity anthologies when authors I know run them (and I can manage it schedule-wise) to support important causes.
>
> And I join some anthologies just for fun because the stories make me happy. I know some people join because being part of a group helps increase read-through to other work, but for me, it's just for fun.
>
> I would caution authors about joining an anthology run by someone who's never done one before or by someone they haven't vetted through word-of-mouth support from multiple authors they trust. That said, people took a chance on me when I ran my first anthology and I'm so glad they did.
>
> Being in an anthology can be epic (like having two anthologies I was included in hit the *USA Today* bestseller list one week after the other!) or terrible. No risk, no reward. I've taken tons of risks as an author, and yes, sometimes I've had a bad experience, but if you're too cautious, you can't move forward.

Joining box sets and anthologies is a great way to accelerate your growth, meet authors in your genre, bring in new readers to your series and backlist, get your letters, and have fun.

"Same old same old" approaches to marketing an anthology

"Same old same old" approaches include inundating social media with posts about the book and asking your email subscribers to pre-order the book every time you mail them.

But certainly, participating authors need to engage their audiences. And if you aren't comfortable with some hardcore marketing, you may not be ready to earn your letters—because the work involved in selling 5,000 or more copies of a title is not insubstantial.

New approaches that have helped push anthology sales

Running ads on Facebook and BookBub, and in other book-promotion emails, can reach new audiences. But keep in mind that in the indie author world, when a group of relatively unknown authors join forces to hit a list, the book they're selling is typically priced at just $0.99.

With royalties of only 30% and a minimum of 15 authors contributing, the most each author can expect to earn, assuming the book sells 5,000 copies, is $100. Buy-in will be at least double that, if not ten times more.

This is why many collections choose to donate all their royalties to a charity, since that $100 per author comes to a total of $1500, an amount that would make a difference to a group doing good in the world. Readers also feel good about buying a book with proceeds going to a charity—assuming they support the cause. It's one of the newer approaches that those hoping to make a run for a list are using that appears to be helpful.

When you join an anthology or boxed set with the goal of earning your bestseller title, it demands both a financial and time investment that is far greater than the hours you put into writing the story you contribute.

Writing for a boxed set

Writing for a boxed set is much the same as writing in a shared world except that the stories share one cover—and the royalties may be differently split.

Recently, eight *New York Times*–bestselling authors at the top of their game—most publicly acknowledge they gross at least a million dollars a year in royalties—each put a full-length novel into a boxed set and gave that eight-book set away for free.

The titles in the boxed set are all available separately from multiple book retailers, and they sell as eBooks for $3.99 to $4.99 each. These titles are also all available as paperbacks and audiobooks.

Why would these A-game authors take books they earn money for and give them away for free? They have two very compelling reasons.

The first is list-building.

All contributing authors promoted the boxed set to their lists. These authors were similar enough that a person who read Author A would likely enjoy authors B, C, D and E. And, to get the free book, readers had to provide their name and email address.

Donna downloaded the book and within a month had welcome emails from those authors she didn't already subscribe to.

Building your email list with readers who enjoy your genre is still one of the most valuable business investments you'll make. It's so valuable that authors who could have been making hundreds (or thousands) of dollars selling a specific title instead bundled it with other popular books to give away—just to get new names on their email lists.

The other reason it makes sense to put full-length novels into a boxed set and give it away is something called read-through.

Seven of the eight titles in the set are the first book in a series of two, three or four books. The odd book out is the second book in a three-book series. These authors, although they are forfeiting their royalties for this first book in their series, are betting that readers will want to continue reading in that world and will go on to purchase the second, third, and fourth books.

These authors understand the cost of advertising. When using an ad platform like Facebook, for instance, you may lose money advertising the first book. But, if your read-through is high, you can still make money on a series. For these authors, giving their first-in-series away for free, and using their peers to promote it, is a lot less expensive than paying for clicks on an ad platform. It will make this boxed set a profitable endeavour.

Case Study: Sofia Aves

Sofia Aves (also writing as Jo Seysener) is an Australian author who, in 2021 alone, contributed to 11 anthologies and wrote 11 full-length romance novels and three picture books. She is a hybrid author—both traditionally and indie published.

Between 2018 and 2021, Sofia—with Jo, her other pen name—has earned 51 publication credits, mostly in anthologies. Her anthology co-author credits are for pieces as short as drabbles (100-word micro fiction) and as long as novellas. The majority of her non-anthology stories run between 30,000 and 80,000 words.

Sofia's first publication credit was in an indie-published anthology with authors in her local writing group. Her next project was her only truly co-authored story, which she wrote with a writer who found her on the Internet and asked if she'd like to co-author Sherlock Holmes fanfic featuring Sherlock as a vampire and Watson as a werewolf.

Sofia had just given birth to her second child, had no idea what she was doing, and co-authored the entire story in Google Docs on her phone while her toddler conducted *Wiggles* concerts and she played with her baby between paragraphs.

That was in 2017.

Since Sofia now writes novels and novellas in three series of her own, one of the reasons she contributes to anthologies is to gain exposure to new readers. If you are considering using an anthology to raise your profile, she recommends signing up early since some anthologies publish stories in the order they receive them. In her experience, it's critical to be one of the first five stories in an anthology to get readers to join your mailing list. And that is a key goal—to grab those readers' names and email addresses so you can let them know when you have your own titles available.

Another major benefit to contributing to anthologies is that those books have limited life spans, typically three to six months. Once the contract has expired and the anthology is no longer available, first rights return to the author, who can repurpose the story.

When Sofia contributes romance stories, she writes a "happily for now" instead of a "happily ever after" ending so that once the anthology commitment is up, Sofia can add more to the story and publish it in her own series world—sometimes as a novella, and sometimes as a reader magnet that's given away for free to entice new readers into her world.

Sofia's advice for authors considering an anthology to grow their readership is to listen to your gut at all stages of the process *before* the writing starts.

The first thing Sofia considers is whether the anthology matches her brand. Submission calls to anthologies typically start with a theme and an already designed cover. If she doesn't have an immediate attraction to both, she passes. But if the theme and cover combination spark a story idea, she'll look at her publication work plan—a detailed spreadsheet of deadlines—to see if a new project will fit the time she has available.

She's had enough experience to recognize if an anthology is being set up well or if it will lead to drama. She doesn't have specific tips about this except to trust your gut.

For an anthology to succeed, every contributor must be an active marketer. So if people are balking at that part of the commitment or it's not clear in the contract—yes, you should read and sign a contract—then look for a different opportunity.

To have marketing reach—the *raison d'être* of an anthology—it has to feature either a couple of powerhouse authors or at least 12 contributing authors.

If you're wondering how the mom of a toddler (and two school-age children) manages to be so prolific, the answer is that she plots out each story and then dictates while she's driving to and from school. She edits her dictations—about 4,000 words in two hours of driving—on the same day she records them.

Your Turn

There's a lot to consider in this chapter, so, if you feel drawn to participating in an anthology or boxed set, take your time with these questions.

- What do you hope to achieve by contributing to an anthology or boxed set? Don't skimp on this question—it's the most important one.
- Are you willing to spend money to participate? If so, how much?
- Are you willing to give up royalties in exchange for status? List-building? Read-through? Your letters?
- Could the requirements of participation compromise your author brand or put your relationship with existing readers at risk?

Once you find an anthology or boxed set that interests you, do your due diligence before you sign a contract or pay to play.

- Ask the set manager for the titles of books from previous sets they've organized.
- Reach out to contributing authors and ask if they'd work with that organizer again, and why or why not.
- Find out the specifics related to your involvement in marketing the collection. Are you able and willing to do that level of promotion?

Here are a few specifics to be aware of.

- Can the contribution be previously published?
- What is the minimum and maximum length of the contribution?
- How long must the contribution be exclusive to the anthology or boxed set?
- Will it be in Kindle Unlimited or published wide?
- Is there an expectation that the contribution will be professionally edited at the author's expense? (This is common.)
- What are acceptable heat, violence, blood and language levels, depending on the genre?
- Can the contribution be a prequel to an existing series?
- Are co-writes welcome or not?
- How many authors will be in the set?
- Is there an anchor author involved—someone who has an established following and reputation?
- How will royalties be split? Will they be paid out to authors or to a charity? If a charity, which one?
- What is the buy-in cost? (For anthologies that are not making a list run, $35–50 is common. For those that are making a run, expect to pay at least $200. For those organized by a traditional publisher there are no costs.)
- Will the anthology manager charge an administration fee? If so, what is it?

- Where and how will the anthology manager communicate with authors, and are you comfortable in that app? Common places are Facebook groups, a Discord channel or a WhatsApp group.
- What is the deadline to submit your publish-ready manuscript?
- What is the publication date of the book?
- How much promotion will you be expected to do? Get specifics about the social media platforms on which you'll be expected to post.

PART III

WHO WILL YOU WRITE WITH?

11

WHAT IS YOUR AUTHOR GOAL?

We've touched on the importance of knowing your author goals before committing to a co-author arrangement. In this section, you'll be asked to think more deeply about your goals and what you want to achieve from your co-authoring experience. Your overall author business goal should be at the heart of all the questions you consider when seeking a co-author.

Once you've thought about your goals, you'll want to discuss them with your co-author to ensure you're on the same page.

Outcome goal

As we pointed out in the first section, Why Do You Want to Co-author Something?, there are many reasons to share the workload of writing a book. But if those reasons, whatever they are, are not in line with your overall goals as an author, there might be another reason why being a co-author seems appealing at first glance.

Writing with a partner can be incredibly rewarding and fun. But like any intimate relationship, it can also be infuriating. It's virtually a given that you and your partner will face at least one moment when you wonder why you ever agreed to this crazy idea of birthing a book baby together. And in that moment—while you remind yourself that clear, calm communication is the cornerstone of all healthy relationships—it's good to anchor yourself to your core author goal.

Here are a few common author goals.

- I want to make enough money writing to quit my day job.
- I want to write and publish three, four, five or more books a year.
- I want the professional credibility of being a published author in my field.
- I want a chance to work with this other author I admire or respect.
- I want to be able to call myself a *USA Today* Bestselling Author.

You may have all of these goals and more. Or you may have one that's not on this list. It really doesn't matter. What does matter is that your primary goal—what we'll call an *outcome goal* in this section—is front of mind as you weigh the pros and cons of tying your wagon to another author's horses and goals.

It's pretty important for you and your co-author to share an outcome goal since you need to be pulling in the same direction. Different goals will cause tension and stress.

For example, if your co-authorship endgame is to make $50,000 a year, and the person you're thinking of working with has the goal of hitting a bestseller list, you may very well find yourself at odds…

- about how much time to invest in the writing and editing of the book;

- about how many books you need to co-author, and in what time frame;
- about how much money to invest in marketing and advertising your co-authored titles.

Process and performance goals

Even if you and your co-author share an outcome goal (what you want to accomplish), you should still have a discussion about two other kinds of goals you'll have en route to success. These are process goals, which you could also think of as strategies (how you do it), and performance goals, which are the standards you set for your shared work (how well you do it).

Here's a fictitious example to help make the point.

Dave and Laura meet at a conference and hit it off. They decide that co-authoring a series would be fun and beneficial. They share the same outcome goal of writing and publishing three cozy mysteries by the time the conference rolls around the next year so they can lead a workshop on how to co-author books. So far so good.

They start working together and find a rhythm that works for them, with Laura writing the first drafts of each chapter and Dave tightening up the scrappy rough drafts and adding deep point of view.

Book one gets finished, and they're both happy with the quality. Laura is anxious to hit *publish*, but Dave believes it would be more strategic to hold on to this book until they've finished the next two. Laura argues that they should publish now so they can start building a readership and make the launch of the second book better.

Both Dave and Laura have good reasons for their strategies and credible examples of authors who've successfully used those strategies. They have a process goal conflict.

They flip a coin, and luck is on Laura's side that day—they hit *publish* and start working on the second book in their series.

Reviews of book one start coming in, and Laura is gutted. Readers are displeased with the amount of swearing in the book and express their displeasure in their reviews and in their stars. Readers prefer their cozies to be a bit cleaner. After 30 reviews, the book has a 3.2 star rating on Amazon; it's even lower on Goodreads.

Dave isn't bothered by the reviews since the book is bringing in over $500 a month in revenue from downloads. Laura wants to address the reviewers' complaints and make the protagonist less of a potty mouth in the next book. Dave argues that the ratings are, at worst, irrelevant and, at best, helping them find their ideal readers—people who like cozy mysteries with an edge.

Now they have a performance goal conflict, and their relationship dissolves during the writing of the second book. Laura wishes Dave luck and lets him finish the series on his own, in his own name.

But Laura, not to be dissuaded from co-authoring, finds another writer to team up with for a different cozy mystery series. She and Joy also set a goal to write three cozies in one year.

After publishing three titles together, Laura attends a webinar. She emerges convinced that taking their series out of Kindle Unlimited and selling wide would be to their benefit. Joy is not a gambler and worries that they won't recoup the money they will lose from KENP page reads, which represents half their income. Laura is looking at long-term sales prospects for these titles, while Joy is thinking about how the next three books will continue to grow their Amazon audience. These are conflicting process goals, since they reflect different strategies one might use to achieve an outcome goal.

Laura and Joy sit down and remind themselves of their original outcome goal: to write and publish three cozy mysteries in a year. "Huh," they say. "We achieved the goal. I guess we need to set a new goal for our published series." They establish a new outcome goal of reaching a wider range of readers with their series.

To do this they use two process goals. First, they will write a prequel and offer it for free to draw in new readers. The second process goal is to pull their whole series out of KU and go wide for two years—the amount of time most experts suggest it takes to build a wide audience.

After two years they agree to review their sales performance and determine if they found an equal or larger readership—and the accompanying income—with the wide sales platform. If not, they'll go back to their Amazon roots.

Understanding the different types of goals

The lesson here is that as an author, you'll have these three kinds of goals—outcome, process and performance—whether you're writing on your own or with a co-author. Start by imagining your desired future as an author, your outcome goal (the what). And then go back to figure out your process goal (the how) and your performance goal (how well).

If you get confused about whether a goal is an outcome, process or performance goal, one way to distinguish them is to understand that your process goals are 100% within your control, your performance goals are mostly controllable, and your outcome goals are out of your control.

Here's one more example to make this point. You set an outcome goal of earning $10,000 in book royalties next year. Your process goal is to write 2,500 words a day, a goal that is entirely controlled by you and how you set your priorities. Your performance goal is to indie publish four titles—this is mostly under your control, but if you hire an editor or cover designer, you will be on their timeline, which is not in your control.

You achieve both of these goals, and you wait for your bank account to increase by $10,000—your outcome goal. But your outcome is not in your control since you can't force people to click the *buy* button. You can do things to make it more likely that they will—write a great book, price the book appropriately, have a professional cover and a good book description, run ads—but ultimately, the decision to buy is not yours.

Your Turn

- What is your *outcome* author goal?
- What does your five-year success look like? Three-year success? One-year success?
- What *process* goals have been proven to help other authors in your genre reach the outcome you seek?
- Is writing with a co-author one of them? If so, what kind of co-author arrangement would work best?
- What process goals are important to you?
- Which process goals are you happy to bend on?
- What *performance* goals have been proven to help other authors in your genre reach the outcome you seek? How many co-authored titles? How many inclusions in anthologies or boxed sets?
- What performance goals are important to you?
- Which performance goals are you happy to bend on?
- Meet with your co-author-in-waiting and discuss your individual outcome, process and performance goals. Are you on the same page? Are you able to negotiate differences?

12

WHAT SHOULD YOU LOOK FOR IN A CO-AUTHOR?

What are you looking for in a writing partner? It's as important a question to answer as "What are you looking for in a mattress?" when it's time to go shopping for a new bed.

Like a new mattress, you want to make sure your writing partner is not too hard (on you), is not too soft (to handle your feedback on their contribution), allows you to work at your best temperature (not too hot or too cold), and lets you sleep well at night (since you might be spending a lot of hours with them every week).

When Donna was co-authoring a book with Tony, she referred to him as her writing husband because there were days she felt like they were married. For better or worse.

And it's not just the amount of time you spend with your writing partner that will make you feel like you've exchanged rings. Just like in real marriage, you'll have disagreements from time to time. Sometimes they'll be small, like, "You changed the protagonist's hair colour again!" to doozies like, "For the hundredth time, we're not writing erotica, so you can't have her do those things you keep putting into Chapter Three. Stop taking off her clothes!"

Despite navigating discussions like these, um, totally fictitious examples, Donna and Tony had a great writing relationship. They were clear on what they could bring to the co-author table and what they wanted and needed the other to bring.

As we discussed in the previous section, knowing your own goals in addition to your partner's goals can go a long way to building a productive and healthy writing partnership that can last a long time.

How much writing experience do you have?

While two co-writers do not have to be exactly matched in their experience, it can be a challenge if they're wildly different. Someone with decades of experience may find it challenging to work with a writer who is just starting out, because they may need to contribute more than their fair share of craft to make sure the book holds together.

On the other foot, a writer with limited experience may feel they have to defer to their co-writer, even when they feel strongly about a story element, because they have less experience or confidence.

Experience in writing and publishing impacts expectations. New people to the field may think, "All we need to do is contact Reese Witherspoon or Oprah and tell them about the book, and we'll have it in the hands of a hundred thousand readers!"

The published author may roll their eyes at this idea; *if only it were that easy*. They may have a stronger grasp on how long things can take in this industry and what is reasonable to expect.

The counterbalance is that someone with less experience is often really excited about the writing process and can help someone more jaded rediscover the fun.

Consider where you are in your own writing journey and what kind of co-author would be a good match for you. If you're unsure, we suggest looking for a partner who is at a similar level of experience and success.

How well do you know the topic of the book?

Imagine you have a great idea for a story but lack experience or knowledge about the topic. Sure, there's Google, and librarians love to help authors, but some books may truly benefit from the depth of knowledge that only first-hand expertise can bring.

A fiction author may have a great kernel of a sci-fi story idea that takes place in a post–climate change apocalypse where the environment is the antagonist. This writer knows she can write the characters, dialogue, emotions, and conflict but feels like she'd benefit from a co-author who can make sure the environment is as worthy and realistic a foe as possible. She finds a writer with a deep understanding of the impacts of environmental change on the planet. Together they write a rich story.

An economist may have a flash of theoretical insight that can be best explained as a metaphor—the evolution of the fairy-tale princess over the last several hundred years. She knows she can write the economics parts, but she doesn't have the insider language of princess life to weave the two ideas together. So she finds a fairy-tale scholar, and together they co-author the most engaging economics book ever written.

How well do you know your potential co-author?

Here's the thing about writing a book with someone. Even if you know that person intimately or have been besties for a decade, you don't know them as a co-author.

It is highly advisable to know your co-author by "dating" them first. Define a short project that you can work on together before you commit to the marriage of a full book. Use this project to see how you deal with disagreements in the story, how well you give and receive feedback, and how much fun you have co-writing with them.

Consider how your different processes work together. Do you need a clear outline to write? Is your co-author a dyed-in-the-wool pantser? Do you write fast and loose and clean it up later, or do you need to go over and over a scene until it is right before moving forward? Do you enjoy when your co-writer takes something you wrote and polishes it, or would you prefer them to write their own chapters?

All three of us have had less-than-successful co-author experiences. Luckily, we all tested the relationships before signing away our happiness on projects that would have driven us to drink vast quantities of cheap wine.

Our success and happiness in creating this series of writing guides together has come about because we respect each other and have found a productive way to work together despite our different writing personalities and creative methods.

How big are the egos in the room?

It seems obvious that it would be a challenge to work in a co-author relationship with a person who has a big ego, who won't listen to feedback, or who can't take criticism because they know best. That person might not listen to your ideas, which would be incredibly disheartening.

But it can be just as frustrating to work with a person who is insecure, who feels hurt by feedback, or who loses confidence as a contributing partner when they get back a chapter that's got entire scenes removed and every word of dialogue rewritten. That lack of confidence can play out in a variety of unhealthy ways, from withdrawing and leaving you to do all the work, to taking on the persona of a Big Ego. This creates an unhealthy working relationship.

How can you know if your potential co-author's ego is *juuust* right? Heck, how can you know how your own ego will act and react in a co-author relationship? We suggest you write something small, maybe the first chapter or two of the larger work, before you make any long-term commitments.

You may also need to consider the dynamics of the relationship. Are you in a co-writing process that is shared equally, or is this a situation where the other author might expect you to ultimately concede to them? Conversely, do you believe this project is "your idea" and that, while you have a co-writer, you expect to be the final decision maker?

It's good to test these things in advance.

What parts of the book writing process do you love—and what would you love not to do?

If you've been writing awhile and have a couple of completed manuscripts under your belt (or under your bed—those count, too), you should have a pretty good idea about the stages of writing and editing that you love and the ones where you get bogged down.

For instance, if you love bashing out a scrappy rough draft and wish a magic fairy would take over once you had the story out, you could look for a co-author who excels at developmental editing.

If you write strong story openings and powerful endings but get hung up in the middle, find an author whose strength is crafting powerfully paced transition chapters. (And then commit that person to you with a blood oath since they are as rare as hen's teeth.)

After working together for a few weeks and several chapters, Donna and Tony found a rhythm that worked for them. Together, they'd brainstorm the upcoming chapter in their story, then Tony would write the first draft. One of his great writing strengths is description, a skill Donna does not share. She'd take his draft and rewrite half of it, tightening the setting and adding dialogue. This way, even though both were working on this project off the sides of their desks, they got through their first draft quickly—in under two months.

What is a hard no? What is a must-have?

Imagine you've taken temporary leave from your day job to get your book written, edited and indie published. You've found someone you think would be a great co-author based on their personality, writing strengths and interests.

What else do you need from that person and relationship? While there is no right or wrong, we've given you some things to consider.

Do you need a commitment that they'll show up every day and meet a completed manuscript deadline?

Or maybe the opposite is true, and your hard no is letting this co-author project interfere with your primary writing goal as an individual author—you want it to be a fun side project that doesn't take over your writing life.

Is your co-author book something you'll be treating like a job, where you show up and do the work whether you're in the mood or not? Or is it a fun project you work on when it fits into your schedule and brings you joy? Or is it something in between?

Are there set skills your co-author must have? A personality type that is a big no?

Co-author, know thyself before you form an intimate bond with another co-author.

Your Turn

- Would you benefit from writing with a person who has expertise you don't? What expertise is that?
- How well do you know your potential co-author *as a* co-author? In other words, have you ever written together?
- What can you do to get to know your co-author at all stages of planning, writing, editing and publishing?
- How well do you and your potential co-author accept feedback on your writing *from each other*?
- What areas of a writing partnership are must-haves for you?
- What areas are hard no's?

13

WHAT CO-AUTHOR QUALITIES WOULD COMPLEMENT YOURS?

Right now you might be thinking, "Holy guacamole, there's a lot of compromise in a co-author relationship."

There can be. But with the right co-author, your compromises could be beneficial to your author career. So who is this magical, mythical perfect co-author? Let's start by having you look at what would make *you* a magical, mythical perfect co-author for someone else. And the biggest piece of that puzzle is understanding yourself.

Are your goals with co-writing pure?

We've talked a lot about goals. There are 101 reasons a person might want to co-author. We'd love to say that there are no wrong answers here, but we've all had negative experiences working on group projects.

Is there something in either your craft or marketing that you feel you are missing but don't want to bother learning?

How is your confidence as a writer? Is a co-author someone who you hope will help you build confidence and make you feel better about calling yourself an author?

Do you want a professionally designed cover and professional editing but lack the budget for them? Do you think a co-author might invest in these for a joint project with you?

If, in your heart, you want to write a book with someone else in order to ride their coattails, effort or bank account to success, we respectfully recommend you hire a ghostwriter instead. It's fine to want to balance out skills or interests, but it's not okay to assume that you won't have to carry your share of the workload or expenses.

Are you a plotter or a discovery writer?

Do you need to have a detailed outline of the story before you start, just a general idea about the characters and the major plot points, or something in between?

If you need a plan and your co-writer likes to wing it, it doesn't necessarily mean a partnership won't work. But you will need to know how you'll work through this difference. Tony is a planner and Donna is not, but they found a good working relationship by meeting often enough for Tony to talk through the plot the way he saw it developing while Donna challenged every plot point with "but why would…" and "but what if…"

This worked because neither author got attached to ideas until they became words. And even then, they never got too attached to the words because if the story was developing in a way that would not serve their outcome goal, they were open to change. We'll come back to this since it's the main reason you don't yet see a book penned by Donna and Tony at your favourite bookseller.

Where are you strongest as a writer?

It's good to know yourself as a writer before you go hunting for someone to complement your stories. One of the reasons Tony and Donna decided to collaborate was to benefit from each other's strengths.

In addition to being able to visualize the main plot points of a story from beginning to end, Tony has great skill writing description and scene setting. Donna, on the other hand, writes first drafts as if the characters are all sitting in chairs on an empty stage just talking and thinking.

Donna's strength and happy place is writing dialogue, which happens to be an area that's less of a strength for Tony.

Their skills complemented each other and helped the co-author team find an easy rhythm for writing first drafts, with Tony starting with the blank page and Donna filling in gaps and giving the characters their deep-point-of-view personalities.

When do you feel comfortable calling a draft done?

If you've ever wondered how many editing passes an author should do before calling their story done, ask that question at one of Donna's Motivation and Accountability Mastermind groups. Most days what you'll find is a range that starts with "I write it, make sure there are no typos, upload it to Amazon or my agent's inbox and call it done" and goes all the way to "I do sixteen different editing passes, each one focused on a different area of the story. Then I give it to beta readers for feedback, make another round of edits and give it to a copy editor. Then I read it out loud one last time and make a few more changes."

Given that both of these approaches are legitimate ways to reach the finish line, knowing where your co-author sits on that very wide spectrum will help ensure you both feel comfortable sending your joint work into the world.

How much time are you willing to spend marketing?

At least one of you will have to invest energy in the work that happens post-publication in order for your book to gain traction. How to get and keep your titles in front of buyers is the subject of many other books, but it's important to know that your book won't automagically sell itself. You and your co-author will need to make decisions about the kind of marketing you'll do, and who will manage the different approaches, before you sign on the dotted line.

Marketing and promotion will be a part of your work whether you go indie or traditional. A traditional publisher will likely have a publicist working on the book with you, but many tasks will still fall to you. If you're indie publishing, there will be even more marketing tasks for you and your co-writer to manage.

How, and how often, do you want to touch base with your co-author?

Face-to-face conversations are critical to success for some writers, even if you and your co-author are writing totally unique sections of a non-fiction book. We know of writing partnerships where all communication takes place via text chat or as notes in a shared writing document, with limited real-time interactions and no meetings in person.

Some writing partnerships will set up a specific schedule of meetings—daily, weekly, biweekly. At certain points in their writing process, Donna and Tony spoke hourly for days.

As a co-author team, Crystal, Donna and Eileen set meetings as needed throughout the process. Since they each had primary responsibility for specific sections in this book, they met (via Zoom) before and after each major draft and revision.

What's your personality type?

Eileen has written an excellent book on how to build better characters that's cleverly called *Build Better Characters*. In that book, she shares a variety of tools from the world of psychology including the 15 measures of emotional intelligence and the Myers-Briggs Personality Indicator. Those tools can also help us understand real-life characters, like ourselves and our possible co-authors.

If you've had experience working in a corporate office environment, you may have had the "fortune" of being put through one or more personality tests that were meant to help you and your colleagues understand how you might behave in different situations.

Donna had this opportunity several years ago when she was subjected to a battery of tests as a manager with a not-for-profit organization. Donna discovered she was a snowflake in her office on the Meyers-Briggs Type Indicator—an introverted, intuitive, feeling, judging personality type. She was also the lone "Red Hat" thinker in an office dominated by "Blue Hats" on the de Bono Six Thinking Hats spectrum.

What does any of this have to do with the price of pork chops in Parksdale? Nothing. But that knowledge shone a light on why Donna worked better, and was happier, with certain teams, and why she was less delighted when she was assigned to work with others. The way different personality types address challenges can foster wonderfully creative solutions with no stress, no mess —or create swirling quagmires of sticky mud that make it difficult to move.

The Six Thinking Hats spectrum is one that's particularly interesting to consider when working with other people. It's intended to be used as a problem-solving tool, where each hat represents a different kind of thinking, a different set of questions. But what's interesting is that as individuals, we tend to approach problems in the hat we feel the most comfortable wearing—*in* our head more than *on* it.

- White hats look at pure facts, figures and information.
- Red hats rely on emotions, feelings, hunches and intuition.
- Black hats are the devil's advocate and love to figure out why an idea won't work.
- Yellow hats bring optimism and dream of opportunities to problem-solving.
- Green hats are always searching for alternatives and innovative ideas and want to move to action quickly.
- Blue hats are the cool thinkers who control the way problems are defined and shape the questions.

Can you see how a person who wakes up in the morning and dons her green hat might find it challenging to work with a blue-hat thinker on all the aspects required to take an idea to publication?

The reality is that we wear all of these hats at different times and in different situations. And all of them are beneficial to creating and managing a successful project. Just knowing your natural hat, and your co-author's, can be enough to stop creative conflict before it starts. It can be as simple as one person saying, "Hey, let's both put on a yellow hat for the next ten minutes and see what we come up with. Then we can try out our black hats to predict obstacles with our different ideas."

If you want to learn more about personality types, we suggest you check out books like these:

- *Emotional Intelligence: Why It Can Matter More Than IQ* by Daniel Goleman, Bantam Publishing, 2005

- *Personality Types: Using the Enneagram for Self-Discovery* by Don Richard Riso, Mariner Books, 2003
- *The Four Tendencies: The Indispensable Personality Profiles That Reveal How to Make Your Life Better (and Other People's Lives Better, Too)* by Gretchen Rubin, Harmony, 2017

Your Turn

- If you're a discovery writer, would you be comfortable writing to a plot that a co-author comes up with?
- If you're a planner, would you be happy to have a co-author challenge your ideas as the story develops?
- In your mind, how good is "good enough" to call a book ready to publish? Describe your preferred editorial process.
- What set of storytelling skills would you most love to have in a co-author?
- What business skills would you most love to have in a co-author?
- What marketing skills would you most love to have in a co-author?
- What storytelling skills do you bring to the co-author table?
- What business skills do you bring to the co-author table?
- What marketing skills do you bring to the co-author table?
- Review your personality and working type by looking at a personality theory of your choice (emotional intelligence, Enneagram, MBTI, etc.).

14

WHAT DO YOU NEED TO KNOW ABOUT YOUR WRITING PARTNER?

As much as you need to know yourself as a co-author before entering a writing relationship, it's equally important to get to know your prospective partner. Here are some of the most important things to learn about your co-author before you dive in.

Level of experience giving and receiving feedback

Experience can make or break a writing partnership. In part, this comes down to skill and writing craft, but inexperience and inflated ego are often bedmates, and a co-author with that combination is someone most of us would want to steer clear of.

Experience with giving and receiving feedback comes down to an understanding of craft but also ego. Someone who is gifted in this area has the ability to identify problems in a manuscript—not just what they would do differently but what might not be working—and is also flexible and open to learning.

If you've got a novel or two—or twelve—under your belt or bed, it's likely your writer's ego has grown and changed as much as your writer's craft through the experience of writing and receiving feedback on your books.

If you're approached by a writer who's drafted a dozen books but has never asked for feedback on their writing, you would be well advised to enter the relationship with a great deal of caution no matter how good their sample pages are.

Working with a co-author is probably not the best way to learn how to receive the sometimes brutal feedback our writing can need.

Imagine working with an author who has written a few books, received feedback on how to improve their story, and flatly rejected the input, believing they know their story better than any editor, agent, publisher or reader ever could.

Self-confidence is absolutely required for an author. You need to know your story and be willing to stand up for what is important to you. However, arrogance, and an ego that can't hear hard truths, are best left at the door. Learning the difference between self-confidence and ego takes time, and it's something you and your co-author must be willing to learn.

Expectations

How do you each work with deadlines?

Do you look at deadlines as mere suggestions? Do they see deadlines as written in stone? That's something you need to sort out before one of you lets a deadline pass while the other skips a family birthday dinner to get the work out on time.

How much of a priority is the co-authored project?

Each of you should make a list of all your priorities and place this shared book in its proper order so you're both aware of what priorities will override your commitment to the book.

If one of you has small children at home while the other has an independent cat, there will have to be an understanding about when keeping tiny humans alive might trump working on the book.

How much time will you commit to this book each week?

Is your expected time commitment in line with the time your co-author commits to the project?

And, if it's not, is it okay for one co-author to invest substantially more time in the book than the other?

Will this be reflected in who benefits—and at what percentage levels—when the royalty cheques start rolling in?

Who will be the project manager?

Anyone who's been through the full process of writing, editing, publishing and marketing a book knows that unless someone is on top of all the details, nothing will get done—or, worse, the wrong things will get done, or things will be done in the wrong order, which will cost time, money or both. And you don't want to be wasting either time or money.

Someone must assume responsibility for each stage, from book idea to collecting royalties.

One of you could be the project manager at the writing stage, and the other could assume the reins when it comes to pitching agents and publishers or handling the minutiae of self-publishing and marketing the book.

Just make sure one of you is in charge of the tasks at each stage.

Set up a project management system

From establishing what time you'll meet each week to sharing files and keeping track of drafts and revisions, you'll need some kind of project management system. Trello, Asana (that's what we use in The Creative Academy for Writers), ClickUp… there are all kinds of systems that can help you stay organized with the 101 (Crystal says 1,001) tasks required to get through the writing, editing, publication and promotion of a book.

Additionally, you'll need a way to track all the decisions you make while in conversation. In the moment, these will feel like decisions you won't forget, but they will, with 100% certainty, be forgotten before you've finished your book. Being able to go back and find answers to questions like "Did we decide to use the Oxford comma or not?" will save you headaches and time when it comes to editing.

Writing down decisions may also reduce potential conflict. It can eliminate the "you said you would" discussion.

Set up a communication system

Donna hates answering her phone so never has her ringer turned on. Crystal takes weekends off and doesn't check email. Eileen likes to keep her evenings free so she can knit and listen to podcasts. (Or have complete conversations with her dogs.) Knowing these things about our communication styles and workday parameters, we set up ways to keep each of us in the loop when important, in-the-moment decisions need to be made.

It took us a few iterations before we found a communication system that kept conversations flowing with the appropriate urgency.

- If something is urgent, we text or phone.
- If someone has a quick question that requires one other person to chime in, a group chat in Discord is our go-to.
- We add decisions that require face-to-face discussion to our Asana work plan, which we all refer to at our monthly meetings.
- A series of shared folders in Dropbox house documents we need to refer to in our discussions.
- Email is a last resort and typically only used to pass

along interesting information when none of the other channels will work.

On paper, as a writing partnership, we have a majority-rules approach to our co-authoring and co-publishing: decisions require only two of the three authors to agree. But in practice, we've never made a decision without all three partners feeling good about it. This means that we sometimes fall into extended conversations while Crystal answers 101 questions about indie publishing approaches in answer to Donna's inner five-year-old asking, "Why?" and Eileen's inner philosopher asking, "What if?" But, ultimately, that extra time and energy is well spent because we can be certain that everyone is on the same page and in agreement before we move forward to the next steps in the process.

However, although so far we've been very lucky not to bump into a conflict that couldn't be resolved, we do have a contract that outlines how to address those issues if and when they arise. Thinking through worst-case possibilities helps us avoid them in the future.

Working style

Are you a laid-back, "go with the flow" kind of person? Is your co-author? Or is she a type-A personality who's always pushing to move faster, harder, stronger?

You don't have to have twin personalities or work styles for a co-author project to succeed, but you absolutely have to know what you are committing to and where your co-author and you may face personality challenges. Because you will. Which is why it's critical to have clear and comfortable communications from day one. (There's more on dealing with conflict in the section How Will You Write Together?)

Your Turn

- Have you lived through feedback and rewrites of your precious words, and killed enough darlings to understand that writing a good book requires checking your ego at the door?
- Has the person you're considering co-authoring with been through this experience?
- Do you want to work with someone who has not yet learned those hard-earned lessons?
- Do you want your co-author relationship to include mentoring a newer writer?
- Do you want to work with an author who has more experience than you have?
- Are you willing to defer to their experience if need be?
- What is your approach to deadlines? Your co-writer's approach?
- Where does this project fit into your list of priorities? How does this match with your co-writer's priorities?
- How much time will you be committing to this project on a weekly basis? How much will your co-writer be committing?
- What system will you and your partner use to track all the details of your project? Who will be responsible for different aspects of the project?
- What is your communication system? Your co-writer's? How will you agree upon a system together?
- What is your working style? What is your co-writer's?

15

WHERE CAN YOU FIND A WRITING PARTNER?

We're not going to provide a list of specific places or sites you can visit to find a writing partner, since that would be overwhelming and would become dated quickly—new places for writers to meet are forming every month.

We will, however, provide a list of the *types* of places you can visit to connect with other people and get recommendations.

Conferences

We wouldn't recommend going to a writer's conference with the sole and express intention of finding a co-author. Something about that feels like going to a nightclub with the sole and express intention of finding someone to share a mortgage with. That said, if you do attend conferences, they can be a fabulous environment in which to get to know people when they're just being themselves, between and after conference sessions.

That's how Donna and Tony found themselves co-authoring. They'd met a number of times at different conferences over a couple of years and were both members of The Creative

Academy for Writers. When Tony proposed a writing partnership to Donna, it was unexpected, but it wasn't like a total stranger was asking her to commit to a writing partnership.

Facebook groups

There are literally dozens of Facebook groups being managed for the sole purpose of helping authors find collaborators. Even if you think what you write is not mainstream enough to find your people, have a look. From paranormal reverse-harem romance to academic research and lots of genres in between, odds are high you can meet other authors looking to collaborate as a co-author or in a boxed set or anthology.

As we mentioned in the section Anthologies and Boxed Sets, these can be a great way to get to know authors' communication styles and writing habits.

Writer groups

In-person writers groups are yet another place to meet and get to know like-minded writers. You can find one on the site Meetup, at annual NaNoWriMo events or at local chapters of many different genre-focused groups, like the following.

- Romance Writers of America (RWA)
- Mystery Writers of America (MWA)
- International Thriller Writers (ITW)
- Science Fiction & Fantasy Writers of America (SFWA)
- Horror Writers Association (HWA)
- Society of Children's Book Writers and Illustrators (SCBWI)

Online communities

It goes without saying that we believe in the strength of finding allies in online communities—this very book is due to the existence of The Creative Academy for Writers. There are numerous online communities out there, many attached to groups that also have in-person events in their local areas. The beauty of online groups is that you can join them from anywhere in the world.

Personal connections

Eileen did career counselling for a number of years. One of her best job-finding strategies was networking. Eileen would advise her clients to tell everyone they knew and met what type of work they were looking to find. At times the people they spoke to directly would know someone. Other times, that person would mention it to someone else they knew, and before you can say "six degrees of Kevin Bacon," an opportunity would be found and a job secured.

If you're interested in co-writing, let other people know. Be as specific as possible. Just as it's not particularly helpful to job-hunt without a focus, it's far more beneficial to tell people in the writing community that you'd like to co-author a reverse-harem paranormal romance or a series of space operas rather than simply "a book."

If you're looking for a co-writer with particular expertise, you may want to reach out to professional organizations or university programs to locate someone who would be a good match.

One of the benefits of having an agent (other than being able to drop "I was talking to my literary agent" into random conversations) is that they are well-connected in the publishing industry. Eileen has been contacted by her agent for opportunities from anthologies to ghostwriting. Her agent is able to share details of the projects, and they discuss how each opportunity might fit into Eileen's personal career goals.

How to approach a potential co-writer

You've decided that you want to co-write with someone. Great! How do you approach them with the idea?

If it's someone you know

The three of us (Crystal, Eileen and Donna) have known each other and worked together for several years. When you're friends or colleagues with someone, the discussion of co-writing can be very casual. Our idea for these writing guides was born over shared drinks and some "what if" thinking. The "invitation" was likely along the lines of, "But seriously... we doing this thing or what? 'Cause we could totally crush this." There's no right or wrong way—as long as your approach fits the relationship you have.

You may choose to approach that person having already thought out the process, but it could also be a brainstorming conversation that leads in this direction.

If it's someone you know of but don't know personally

If you are reaching out to a writer you don't know, you'll likely need to be a bit more formal in your approach. You'll need to introduce yourself, describe your writing and publishing experience, and explain why you're interested in working with them in particular.

No one wants to think you want to partner with just *any*one. This is not a time to say "Dear Writer." You want to make that potential partner feel special. You'll also want to outline in at least broad strokes what type of project you are seeking and why you want to work with *them* in particular.

If it's an existing shared world with a track record

To join an existing shared world as a co-author, there will almost always be an application process. Check the website for a shared world you're interested in to see their expectations and requirements.

If it's a boxed set, anthology, or a new shared world

By way of example, here's a fun fact about how many story collections organically come to life.

In a Facebook group that caters to authors who are interested in co-authoring, one person will post something like

> I'd like to write a book where women who are thrown off ships for being bad luck magically evolve into mermaids who then sing the ships toward rocks, drowning all the sailors on board.

A story idea very much like that one had a dozen authors post to say they'd like to write that kind of story. And so the conversation between interested parties starts, usually in a new Facebook group just for those interested in that collection.

Some boxed-set organizers have Google Docs that list their open anthologies and include a sign-up form. You'll find these in the Facebook groups that cater to sets.

If it's a big-name author or a book packager

In these cases, there's likely a formal application process, and you're more likely to be successful going through that individual's agent or publisher.

Your Turn

- Are you clear about what kind of co-author relationship will be best-suited to your outcome, performance and process goals?

- Write up a concise author-seeks-author ad that describes your writing and publication experience; your author strengths (craft, editing, business, marketing); the kind of project you'd like to co-author (specific genre, book format); your desired publication date for the co-authored work; the experience, strengths, skills and personality type of your ideal co-author.
- You may post that "ad" in a group, but it's most useful as a tool to help you vet potential co-authors you have conversations with.
- Make a list of every author in your desired subgenre with whom you have a direct or one-person-removed connection. Send them a brief message saying you're looking for a co-author. Ask if they have ideas.

PART IV

HOW WILL YOU WRITE TOGETHER?

16

WHAT KIND OF A BOOK ARE YOU CO-WRITING?

Before you head down this co-writing road, you and your co-authors need to be clear on exactly what kind of books you're writing, and who you're writing them for.

Identify your genre and subgenre, if appropriate

It's not enough to decide that you and your co-author will be writing a romance novel. You need to know, before you start plotting or writing, how much steam that story will have. If it's a fantasy, how out-of-this-world your world will be, or if it's a thriller, how many litres of blood will be spilled.

Think about your main characters and what kind of heroes and heroines you feel comfortable writing and having in your author backlist.

Consider the settings you feel most confident writing about. If, for instance, you've always lived in a small town and that's what you know but your prospective co-author sets every story they write in New York City, how will that work? It's not that it can't work, but it's a creative question to nail down before you get too far into the relationship.

It's also one that will come up when you're editing. Since one of you will have more experience than the other, it would make sense that their word would carry more weight when it comes to creative negotiations.

Stacey Wallace, who is co-authoring a series of screenplays for television and movies with a long-time friend and actor, says that their partnership gives them each areas where their experience trumps the other's opinions. And, although it's sometimes hard to accept, they know how to ease each other into letting go of darlings that might work in one context but aren't the best fit for their joint projects.

Identify your audience

Identifying your audience is one of the best ways to determine how you and your co-author can be stronger together. One of the benefits of co-authoring is being able to build your readership by bringing your co-author's readers to your list. This isn't to suggest that you won't find overlap if you write steamy romance and your co-author writes thrillers, but it may be more of a challenge than if you're already attracting the same kinds of readers.

But stepping way beyond the expected can be productive. Evidence for this is the recent co-author partnership between James Patterson (best known for his thrillers) and Dolly Parton (yes, *that* Dolly Parton). It may seem like an odd pairing, but the story they're co-writing makes sense. The fact that both authors have a strong commitment to supporting children's literacy is perhaps the magnet that will hold these two quite different creatives—and their audiences—together.

Identify the parameters of your book

You need to identify the scope of your book. This seems obvious, but the more specific you can be the better.

In addition to knowing your genre and the expectations that go with it, consider early on the length of the book you're co-writing, the point of view, whether your co-authored book will be a one-off or the start of a series, and so on.

If your plan is to co-author non-fiction, it can help to read other books in the subject area and learn from them as you develop your own spin.

When the three of us decided that we wanted to launch The Creative Academy Guides for Writers, we each read (or re-read) several other writing guides, with two main questions in mind:

1. What worked well in those other books?
2. What would we have done differently?

For example, we agreed to have a call to action at the end of each chapter in our books because we all found books that forced us to bring their general advice to our specific situations to be the most useful. Thus, the Your Turn sections were born.

We also recognized that, while some very good guides for writers are quite formal and read almost like academic texts, we were more comfortable writing in a more conversational tone.

Defining these two core parameters for our series has ensured they fit together as a whole, despite the different voices in our single-author titles.

Pin down your ideas

Just as there are dozens of different ways to start a book you write on your own, there's no one perfect approach to outlining your co-authored story. How detailed an outline you create will be in part determined by how you decide to write together.

For instance, if your plan is to co-write in real time, either in person or online on video, you could get away with an outline that's as detailed as asking "Where do we go next?" each time you meet.

But if you're both writing on your own—for instance with you writing the chapters in the heroine's point of view and your co-author writing the hero's point of view—it's important to make sure your outline has enough direction to ensure you're both headed toward the same destination. You don't want to get pages back from your co-writer and discover that they've added an unexpected serial killer to your book. (This can happen if you write with Eileen. Look, she's doing it right now!)

In the Writing Excuses podcast "Barbie Pre-Writing" (season 15, episode 29), co-authors Janci Patterson and Megan Walker describe the way they start every book they've written together—which is over 20 to date.

As the title suggests, Janci and Megan use Barbie dolls to role-play their entire storyline before they actually start writing. In what they call their Barbie Room, they have multiple dioramas (scenes) and full costuming, which they use as they *become* the hero and heroine of their romance stories. The episode is absolutely worth a listen.

But don't worry if you got rid of your Barbies years ago or role play isn't your thing. You can brainstorm ideas in any format that works for you and your co-authors. If you're looking for tools to help, there are many options:

- Mind-mapping software such as MindMeister or MindNode
- Scapple or Plottr to capture ideas

And if analog tools like a notepad, sticky notes, notecards or a giant whiteboard are your preference, there's no shame in that. As long as you can share what you create with your partners as needed, you're golden.

Your Turn

Get as specific as you can about the subgenre of book you'd like to co-author.

- How will that genre support your broader author goals?
- Is it a genre your existing readers will enjoy?
- If not, will you write under a pen name?
- What will the marketing implications of creating a new author persona be to your author business?

What story and broader book parameters are important to you?

- How long a story are you willing and interested in co-authoring?
- Do you envision this book as a one-off? The start to a series?
- Will the book be written in one point of view or more?
- Will the story be told in first or third person?

What specific creative ideas do you have about a co-authored book?

- Start by identifying the expectations of readers of your chosen genre. If it's romance, you know you need a happily ever after. If it's young adult, kids will be the stars and adult characters will be background noise for the most part. If it's self-help, there will be calls to action.

- Now get more specific about what interests you. Do you want your female protagonist to have a specific quirk or quality? Do you need your hero to have a specific core wound? Does the setting of your story need to include a secret room behind a wall in the family home?
- What tools do you like to use for brainstorming?
- What published books do you consider comparable to what you'd want to co-author? What elements are similar? What elements would you do differently? Has your potential co-author read these books, and do they agree with you?

17

HOW WILL YOU WRITE THAT BOOK?

The next few sections will start answering the question of how you will write that book—the systems or processes you could use, and the tools that will help you get from brilliant idea to completed manuscript.

Agree on a writing process

It may seem a bit backward to define a writing process before you agree on an outlining process, but in fact it is critical to do it in this order. The way you outline and the depth of detail you need are going to vary dramatically depending on how you and your partner(s) plan to write the book. Let's dig into a few different approaches to co-authoring.

We're going to use Writer A and Writer B here for simplicity, but the ideas stay the same even if you add writing partners.

Shared-world or shared-series style

If you're writing in a shared world, or a series with characters that tie the stories together, then partners don't need to agree on how they'll write and outline their contribution.

Author A writes her own story. Author B writes his own. Each author can write their book however the heck works best for them and their process.

One thing the authors do need is a shared document that lists the anchor characters, settings and event timelines that are required to be included in each other's books.

The shared world in which Donna wrote was created by author Rebecca Norinne. It featured a well-developed college campus and adjacent town with a pizza parlour where students hung out. The setting, as described by Rebecca, was New England—not a state, not near a specific real city—just New England.

Donna and a couple of other authors fumbled on this important detail by mentioning specific location details in their stories. Guess who was editing her book in the hours before the Amazon upload cut-off time?

Relay style

Relay style describes a process in which Writer A drafts a chapter then hands it off to Writer B. Writer B reviews and edits the chapter then continues by writing another chapter. They pass the manuscript back to Writer A, and the process repeats.

Relay style can work with any number of POV characters, regardless if everyone is writing all the characters or specific people have claimed certain POV voices.

If you are using a relay style, while it might help to have some sense of major plot points or character development, it's not strictly necessary. Relay style co-writing can follow the rules of improv theatre—no blocking, and always saying, "Yes, and…" each time it's your turn to write a chapter.

It's like a fun discovery game. This method requires a lot of trust between co-authors, and potentially a bit more editing to iron out plot issues down the line. But it may be a good option when you have a team comprised entirely of discovery writers (also called pantsers).

This is the approach that Mia Harlan and five other writers took when they co-authored *Love Blooms*. Mia and Eva Delaney plotted the story and assigned chapters to the other authors. Hanleigh Bradley took on the role of time manager, which meant she was the whip who kept everyone honest and on schedule with their chapters. Mia said it was a fun experience.

Parallel style

In a parallel-style writing process, Writer A and Writer B work simultaneously on different scenes, point of view sections or, in non-fiction, different chapters and topics.

If you're writing simultaneously, you'll probably need at least a rough idea of what is supposed to happen in each scene—so you know what comes right *before* the scene you're writing or what comes *after* the turning point you're writing toward. Think of it like fitting together two puzzle pieces. They need complementary edges in order to fit seamlessly.

You and your writing partner will also benefit from a style guide or story bible to track key details and ensure you're being consistent throughout the story.

Marathon relay style

Marathon relay style is what we are calling it when two writers take turns with the whole manuscript or, at the very least, substantial sections.

Writer A bangs out a scrappy rough draft then hands it off to Writer B. Writer B goes through the manuscript with an eye to doing a first-pass edit—fleshing out characters, tightening up dialogue, developing more drama around existing plot points, and adding scenes if required. Then Writer A gets it back to do their thing.

This approach requires a great deal of trust and respect between co-authors, since darlings might be killed while the manuscript is in the care of the other writer. We'd suggest this as an advanced co-author approach.

When the completed manuscript needs a little—or a big—something

Sometimes a writer will get to the end of their manuscript and think, "I want something different" or "I need something more."

It may not be very common for a writer to hand a "complete" manuscript over to another writer and ask them to add to it, but it happens.

Stacey Wallace wrote this way. Her co-author had a completed memoir that, on reflection, she decided she'd like to publish as a romance. Since she'd written the memoir in the first person, Stacey was tasked with writing alternating chapters in the hero's point of view.

Donna had an almost completed manuscript but was left with one finicky problem to overcome—her steamy romance story had spots that said "[INSERT SEX SCENE HERE]." Because she had no desire to jump into bed with her characters, she brought in a trusted author friend to help out.

Outlining processes (or lack thereof)

For some fiction authors, a detailed outline can be the kiss of death for their creative process. But having at least a rough idea of what you are going to co-write is kind of important. It lets each partner know which parts of the story they'll be responsible for.

If you are working with authors who like to draw detailed outlines and that works for you all, that's fabulous. But if you're using one of the methods above that requires co-operative and overlapping storytelling, have a conversation about how your co-author outlines.

If you outline using a specific tool, method or approach—the Snowflake Method, *Save the Cat*, a genre-specific beat sheet, or the method from *The Plot Whisperer*—your vision of an outline and the outlining process may or may not be compatible with the way your writing partner generally does it.

This is not to suggest that having different approaches will be a problem, but it's important to pick a method that works for both (or all) of you.

For non-fiction writers, narrowing down what will be included in the table of contents (and who will tackle which parts) will get you on your way to that first finished draft and save you a ton of time in the editing stages.

When we co-author books in the Creative Academy Guides for Writers series, we start by brainstorming our outline as a group. We create a shared document with the bare bones and then, over a set period of time, fill in gaps and iron out a topic order we think makes sense. That document becomes our outline.

Once we have this, we divide up the sections based on interest, knowledge and background. Then we write our sections in the order they'll appear in the final book, handing over drafts to the author of the next chapter or section. This approach saves us time and energy in the editing stages since it helps us avoid writing overlapping content.

Your Turn

- Review how each person in the group likes to write. What kind of writing process do you think will work best for your partnership?
- What style of book or story outline is everyone in your co-author partnership comfortable with?

18

WHAT WRITING TOOLS WILL YOU USE?

By this point, you should have had plenty of conversations with your co-author and have figured out roughly how you want to work together. Formalizing your process will help you choose your writing tools. It will also help you develop systems to ensure you're on the same page and to avoid conflict and confusion.

Below, we've broken down a few tools that help streamline some of the most common co-writing processes. We've also included some key questions for you to answer with your writing partner.

Why did we put systems first? Why not start with tools? It's because we want you to choose the tools that will support the writing process you know, like and trust. While there may be some give and take, there's no reason to remake your writing process to fit a tool—there are apps and solutions to fit just about any set of writing preferences.

You'll need to decide on a system and tools for three different stages of the writing process.

1. Brainstorming and outlining
2. Writing
3. Editing

Tools for writing at the same time

As we detailed in the previous section, some co-authors work on their project simultaneously. While this is a great way to move a project forward quickly and allow each author to work at their own speed, the approach can have its challenges.

It requires some good collaborative outlining so everyone knows where and how the manuscript and story are going to come together.

This can work well in fiction where each author writes their own characters or chapters from their own point of view. It's also a good fit for non-fiction projects where each author-expert has specific sections they will write.

Brainstorming and outlining tools

If you and your co-author want to work on a document simultaneously and be able to read each other's writing, Google Docs is great for brainstorming and outlining.

If you want to work simultaneously but do not need to see what your co-author is writing, your own word processing software will work just fine.

When writing the first draft of any of our co-written Creative Academy Guides, we brainstorm the outline of the book together to determine what topics we'd like to cover and what questions we want to answer. We usually dump ideas in a Google Doc together live, and then everyone contributes new ideas and thoughts over a set time period before we nail down our final outline.

Writing and editing tools

Once we've agreed on what to include in our co-authored book, we group the topics into sections. Then we—we being Crystal—put them together into a nicely shaped outline using Scrivener. Each section is highlighted in a specific colour that denotes which author is responsible for the content.

At that point, we—Crystal!—replicate the file so each of us has her own Scrivener project to work from. We tend to keep these individual files in a shared Dropbox folder so we can check in on each other's work as needed. For this book, Donna wanted to reference Eileen's first few chapters before starting her own, since she was also going to touch on the upsides and challenges of co-authoring models and didn't want to duplicate what Eileen had already written.

Once we've all finished drafting our own sections, one of us (ahem, you know who) combines the three files into one master Scrivener file. And then we each have a turn reviewing and revising that master file. It goes from author to author until we've dealt with all the comments, questions, suggestions and blank spots.

Final editing tool

At that point, the file is exported to a Word document, the formatting is cleaned up, and then it's sent off to our editor for proofreading.

Tools for relay writing

With relay writing, only one author works on a manuscript at a time before handing off to their co-author. In this situation, there is a great deal of flexibility regarding tools because you can use email or a cloud drive to share the file back and forth. As long as the word processing program you use works for your writing partner, you're golden.

Word processing tools

Word processing options include Google Docs, Word, Scrivener, Pages, Ulysses and Final Draft. Which word processing program you choose will depend on what each author is comfortable with and what you may already own.

When the three of us began working together, both Donna and Crystal loved using Scrivener. Eileen was used to Word. When we decided that Scrivener made sense—and its tidy, colour-coordinated outline view on the side made Crystal beyond happy—we built in some time for Eileen to become comfortable with the system. You'll need to build in this time if someone is learning a new system. You'll also need to make sure that all team members have compatible versions of the software—some are specific to Macs or PCs, and some software updates "break" older versions.

Shared cloud drives

Google Drive, Dropbox, iCloud, and One Drive all allow you to store documents in one location where all co-authors can access them.

While our team members write in their own documents in the crafting stage, we house the files in a shared Dropbox folder. This allows us to check in on what others are doing if we have questions as we progress.

Your process will likely evolve as your writing process and partnership evolve. Building in time to reflect upon and discuss what's working and what might be frustrating is just as important in your writing relationships as it is in your romantic partnerships.

Your Turn

- Discuss the pros and cons of working on the same document at the same time versus working on separate documents.
- What writing software are you most comfortable or familiar with?
- What writing software is your co-author most comfortable with?
- Are you willing to learn something new if it makes sense to the co-author approach you're using? If not, is your partner?
- If there are tools you both use that will work for your chosen approach, are you using the same versions?
- If one of you writes on a Mac and the other on a PC, are there any issues that come with swapping files between the two?
- If your team is going to use a new tool, how much time will each person need to become comfortable with at least the basics?

19

WHAT COMMITMENTS ARE YOU MAKING?

In order to make a strong writing commitment together, you and your co-authors will have to establish shared guidelines and agree on a few important things—like goals, time and money—before you dive into your project.

Agree on a performance goal

Earlier we touched on how important it is to identify your career goals as an author and to understand where your co-author projects fit into your broad writing career.

Has your co-author done this work as well? It's very important to make sure that you both can agree on a performance goal for your shared project(s) that supports what you're each trying to achieve in your careers.

This is not to suggest you have to have identical career goals or outcome goals. You absolutely do not—but they do have to be aligned.

Take our co-author team of three for example.

Eileen's outcome goal is to make $10,000 a month entirely from writing non-fiction (hey, spendy handbags don't buy themselves). Donna's outcome goal is also to be earning $10,000 in book royalties a month but through an equal split between her fiction and non-fiction writing. Crystal's focus is on fostering balance in her life while increasing her income by $250 each month for the next two years, through a mix of fiction and non-fiction revenue streams.

Our individual outcome goals are not the same. And that's fine because we all agree on the shared performance goal of adding four high-quality and helpful Creative Academy Guides for Writers to our series in the coming year. Unlike our income, that's a goal we control and one we can work toward together in addition to our individual projects.

So, although your outcome goal doesn't have to be the same as your co-author's, your performance goal does. Your outcome goal influences the choices you make, which then lead to performance.

Using the example above, since we all have ambitious income goals, the work required to publish four titles keeps our performance goals aligned. But if one of us didn't care about royalties from our non-fiction series, it could create complications or conflicts.

Agree on a timeline

Once you've agreed on a performance goal, it's much easier to set a timeline for the steps that need to happen to achieve those goals.

Timelines are tricky. Life happens—usually at the most awkward possible moment—and we need to be able to adapt and flex to fit life's bumps in the road. Each additional writing partner introduced into a book's mix increases the potential for complications and delays that could impact the project timelines.

On the flip side, having co-authors can alleviate stress if tasks or timelines need to be juggled.

It's important to discuss best case and worst case scenarios with your writing team—to play the what-if game as it relates to all the things that could get in the way of meeting a co-writing obligation.

It's also important to understand the personalities and habits of the people you're working with so you can play to everyone's strengths and use each author's super powers to the max.

Know how you and your co-author respond to deadlines

Creatives are an interesting breed. If you put ten writers in a room and tell them they have a drop-dead deadline to get a piece of work written, you can expect a few to get to work immediately and have the draft ready for an editor early. A few will plug away a bit every day until the project is complete, and at least one will be slower to put their butt in the chair but who will then write like that chair is on fire.

Understanding how your co-author relates to deadlines is critical because if you don't have the same kind of deadline drive, that difference might drive you crazy. Is there a way to work effectively with a person who is different than you? Absolutely!

In our partnership, Eileen is the author who works steadily toward her deadline from the day it's set. She doesn't like to be rushed, so she's a great person to get things started on our co-authored projects. Donna does well when she has a very specific deadline to hand work over to someone else. She doesn't want to let anyone down, so she fits nicely in the middle of our writing process. And then there's Crystal, who thrives on hard and immovable deadlines like a pre-order date or a commitment to get the book to the editor. Crystal is usually the last person to work on drafts in our co-writing process.

Be realistic about your commitments

When we're about to embark on a new collaborative title for our series, we discuss when we'd like to see that book out in the world. This tells us when we'd need to have different drafts done.

Then we talk about what else is going on between now and then, like what's happening in our personal lives (moves, family visits, health stuff), planned holidays and long weekends, our independent creative projects and anything else that will take us away from our desks.

Why spend time discussing stuff that doesn't have anything to do with our shared project? Because the commitments we've made to our family, friends, and our own creative work will impact how attentive we'll be to our shared project. Seeing the big picture in each other's lives allows us to look after each other.

While some people prefer to keep things all business, we've learned that when it comes to our creative partnership, knowing what other forces could impact our writing partners' creativity can be invaluable. This doesn't just make us nicer people—it makes us a stronger team able to identify and amplify each other's strengths.

And, of course, nobody plans to be flooded out of their home or to move twice in 12 months… but that's the kind of life stuff that happens. Having conversations about non-writing commitments helps us anticipate changes to our team's schedule before a missed deadline causes problems.

Set reasonable deadlines

A writer has just contacted you to co-author a story for an anthology that's doing a run for the *USA Today* bestseller list. The snag? The book will be published in six weeks, and you'll have ten days to co-write a 20,000-word novella. The deadline is immovable. Do you drop everything to take on this challenge?

The first thing you should consider—aside from whether your family or pets will forgive you if you disappear into your writing cave for the next ten days—is how well the project fits with your career goals.

Ten days may not seem like a reasonable deadline—unless one of your goals is to be a *USA Today* Bestselling Author and that anthology has some heavy hitters and a solid chance of making the list.

Mia Harlan was put in just this situation. For a week, she put aside everything else she was working on. A month later, she had her letters. It was a gamble that made sense for her author career goal.

What about books where you control the deadlines? Smart writing teams build in time buffers to account for unexpected setbacks and the reality of each author's work process.

For example, when Eileen is planning her own books, she starts by doing some math that looks like this...

- Know that my average novel is 75,000 to 80,000 words
- Assume I will write 7,000 to 10,000 words a week
- Pull out my calculator and determine it will take 8 to 12 weeks to write my book
- Laugh hysterically
- Remember that I will throw out at least half the words of my scrappy rough draft
- Recalculate deadline to 12 to 18 weeks out
- Assume at least a week off in those months for a holiday, another week for odd emergencies, a week to deal with writer's block or extra research...
- Recalculate, and admit I need 15 to 21 weeks to finish a solid first draft of a new novel

It would be silly for Eileen to agree to a 13-week deadline for a draft unless she were willing to spend more time writing more words each week, forgo a holiday, give up her social life—or not have writer's block!

Remember Sofia Aves, the author who contributed to 11 anthologies and wrote 11 full-length romance novels and three picture books in 2021?

One might wonder how an author who basically writes a book every other week manages their deadlines. The answer is… with an Excel spreadsheet.

Here's some of what Sofia tracks, as it relates to deadlines.

- Name of the anthology or series
- Title of the story
- Story tag line
- Word count limits
- Deadline to submit edited manuscript
- Launch date

And then Sofia makes note of each book that has a process deadline that month, placing the closest deadline in the first spot. The items at the end of the month may only be partially completed if they aren't due. They are then bumped to the front of the following month.

This is an example of one month on Sofia's deadline spreadsheet.

Book A: finish edits

Book B: write 30K words

Book C: write 12K words

Book D: write 5K+ words

Book E: write 8–10K words

Book F: write 30K+ words

You can see from Eileen and Sofia's real-life examples that the there is no one way to set reasonable deadlines for your co-authored (or individual) books. But there are ways to figure out what you can feasibly do given your work style, the length of your stories, and so on.

Agree on a budget

Yeah, we know. Numbers, math and money aren't always an author's favourite topics. But you and your co-authors need to be clear on how much you're each able and willing to invest in your project during the writing, publication, and marketing stages of your book's life.

Your Turn

First, let's focus on setting some goals and timelines for your project.

- How does each member of your team respond to deadlines? How can you adapt your process to make these different approaches work *for* you?
- What is your shared project's performance goal?
- What is an ideal timeline for this project?
- Does your project have a "drop dead" completion date? If it does, walk yourself backwards from that date. When would you like to have completed your outline? First draft? Revisions? Have you built in buffers for unexpected time sinks?

Now turn your attention to some budget and money questions.

- How much money are you willing to invest in new writing software to make this co-author project run more smoothly?
- How much will you invest in apps, programs, and software at the research and writing stage?
- How much will you set aside for an editor?
- How much for marketing?

20

HOW WILL YOU ENSURE CONSISTENCY AND SAFETY OF BACKUPS?

We talk about systems for backing up your work in all of our Creative Academy Guides for Writers. You work darn hard to get your words out of your head, and when working on a collaborative project the risk of accidentally overwriting your work is much higher than the risk of losing work that only you have access to.

Once you've figured out what writing and editing software you're going to use, and your process for using those tools, we highly recommend that you include a step to regularly back up drafts of your work.

What's that? It's in the cloud, so you're totally good on this point?

Yeah, you'd think so. But even files in the cloud can be corrupted or accidentally deleted. What if your writing partner's three-year-old wants to help Daddy type his book and accidentally hits *delete*?

Yes, Google drive has an option to dial back to a previous version. And, yes, if you are paying for the professional version of Dropbox, you will have 30 days to recover files deleted by mistake—or misunderstanding.

But even so, it's smart to save multiple copies of your work-in-progress in at least one additional place in case something goes awry.

How do we suggest you do this? It depends on the tools you use and the process you have. But just so you have some examples of how it *could* work, we'll share our systems from a few different collaborations. One of these options may work for you and your co-author.

Writing in separate documents within a shared folder

If you're using Word or Google Docs, you can create a shared folder for your book and write each chapter as a separate document within the folder. This mimics the way Scrivener works, with each chapter or scene as its own file.

Using this approach, co-authors can easily access any chapter or scene that their partner doesn't currently have open. This also helps you avoid the issues that arise with Google Docs, which has an upper limit on the number of edits or corrections that can exist in a single document.

Taking turns writing in a shared document

Create a backups subfolder in a shared cloud folder. When you start work each day, duplicate your file and save a new copy with the current date. Work in the file with today's date and move the previous version into your backups folder. This approach works well in Google Docs as well as other cloud destinations.

Scrivener

Scrivener backups can be saved to a cloud-hosted folder or a local drive. It's important to know where your file is being saved when you co-write. If you're each saving your day's work to your local drive... you'll have headaches. Make sure to select the cloud backup option. But if you're doing this with a shared file, make sure only one of you has it open on your desktop at a time or it can cause problems.

Regardless of which option you use to back up your co-written words, agree on (and stick to!) a standardized file-naming convention. Using words like *final* in your file name is a bad idea which we admit we know first-hand. *Is the upload version called* FinalFinal *or* FinalforReal? Don't put yourself in that situation!

Wanting never to repeat that stressful experience, we agreed to use the following naming system for our co-written books.

For example, we named our files for this book with the title, our initials, *Blended* to indicate it contained copy from all three of our individual files, and then the month and day.

CreateWithCoAuthors-C+D+E Blended-0709.scriv

CreateWithCoAuthors-C+D+E Blended-0729.scriv

CreateWithCoAuthors-C+D+E Blended-0817.scriv

Once the we moved to the last stage of revisions, we changed the naming convention to indicate which one of us was actively editing the file. The date was critical to knowing which version was the most current.

CreateWithCoAuthors-Eileen-0819.scriv

CreateWithCoAuthors-Crystal-0827.scriv

CreateWithCoAuthors-Donna-0907.scriv

Your Turn

- Which backup method will you use?
- Where will you store backups?
- How often will you back up your file(s)?
- Will you keep all backup drafts, or will you delete archived versions?
- What is your file-naming convention? (Be sure to include the manuscript name or abbreviation, the co-author name or initials, and a date format that goes year, month, day so that your files will sort themselves in chronological order!)

21
HOW CAN YOU SHARE A WRITING WORLD?

In collaborations that involve writing in a shared world, you may have characters that appear in multiple books, locations that need to be consistent, and other elements that tie the titles together.

Contributors may have to agree on many elements of the stories, set boundaries and limitations around what already exists in worlds that have a history, and establish what can be changed, added or destroyed by an individual author.

In the shared world that Donna joined, the world creator shared a Google spreadsheet with a few details about the town, a map of the college campus, and the names of characters who'd appeared in the first two books in the series. It took less than five minutes to review and understand it.

By contrast, the world that Mia Harlan created in Silver Springs has a bible hundreds of pages long, with details about the characters, locations and other elements that have appeared in more than 70 books in the four interconnected series.

Even if you and one co-author are writing your first book together, you're writing in a shared world. To help you get off on the right foot, we brainstormed a list of story questions to consider. You can download an editable version of this Shared Writing World Questionnaire Google Sheet from CreativeAcademyForWriters.com/resources.

Brand and genre

- What kinds of stories can be written in this world? Think subgenre, tone (dark, light, gritty, fun) and time period (contemporary, historical, future).
- How long are stories in this world? Are they flash fiction, short stories, novellas, short novels or full-length novels, and what are the required word counts for each of these?
- How complex are the plots? (In part, story length will dictate this.)
- What are the world must-haves for each book? A dead body? A strong female protagonist? A wounded hero? A community meeting place? A happily-ever-after? A cat that solves mysteries?
- What are the world rules that can't be broken? Can spells only be cast on Fridays? What words are considered swear words? Does sex only happen behind closed doors?

Characters

- Are there characters who should appear in every story, assuming a series or multi-author shared world? Do you have descriptions of these characters—their looks, their personality, and the roles they fill?
- What kinds of characters can be brought into the world?
- Who is permitted to add new characters to the world?
- When new characters are added, are they included in the

shared-world bible or do they remain as part of the individual author's story only (i.e., do new characters cross over from book to book)?
- Who owns new characters brought into an existing world?
- Can shared characters appear in stories written outside the collective world, series or set of books?
- Can shared characters be killed off or changed in a significant way?

Events

- What significant events are part of this world's history?
- Are there timeline restrictions for stories added to the world? Can a story be written at a date that obviously precedes an already-published story? Can a story be written long into the future?
- Are there timeline restrictions for significant events that get added to the world?
- Are there restrictions on the types of events you can add?
- How will new events impact existing or future stories?
- How are new events tracked in the shared-world timeline?

Settings

- What settings are in the world?
- What descriptions exist of these settings?
- Can new settings be added to the world?
- Can locations be destroyed or removed?
- Do maps of buildings, towns, cities, countries or worlds exist?

Your Turn

- If you're building a new world with a co-author, schedule a few hours to brainstorm questions like the ones above. You don't need to have all the answers when you start, but establish a general direction and create a shared document, adding new information as you get to know your world.
- If you're joining an existing world, your leader will likely provide you with the details they feel are important to maintain consistently through stories. Follow those guidelines to the letter.

22

HOW DO YOU RESOLVE CONFLICTS IN THE WRITING PROCESS?

Has it been stated too many times yet that working with a co-author is not that different from having a spouse?

Compromises will need to be made—that's a given. The question is how to reach agreement without straining your relationship. We feel the issue of conflict is so important that we're discussing it here in the writing section and again in more detail in the section How Will You Handle Conflict?, which relates to the publishing business.

Talk early and often

Regardless of the relationship's power dynamic and agreed-upon work systems, all partners need their voices to be heard. Even if one of you has more experience or is covering a higher portion of the expenses, co-writing is a partnership, and both parties must be comfortable expressing themselves at all times. That includes asking questions and expecting non-snarky answers.

Know your conflict style

As writers, we love conflict—the more the better. Eileen likes conflict so much she wrote a whole book on how to make more of it, called *Create Story Conflict*. Even though conflict is a healthy part of any relationship, it's not a top-priority activity for most people.

If you haven't already, examine your own conflict style.

Do you avoid it, or do you enjoy a good debate?

When you're upset, do you become passive, aggressive, or passive-aggressive?

Do you find yourself saying, "Everything's fine," and then feeling hurt when the person who has upset you can't tell that you're very much *not* fine?

Do you tend to give in when conflict occurs?

We're not here to make judgement about how you deal with conflict, but having a heart-to-heart with your co-author about your typical responses to feeling unheard or upset—*before* you find yourself in a tricky situation—can go a long way to speeding up resolution.

Pinpoint the source of your disagreement

Sometimes, the best way to approach something you can't agree on is to take a step back and make sure your disagreement is about the right thing. If you and your co-author are looking at a scene, for instance, and are unable to agree on whether the hero wins or loses the mini battle, perhaps the right question to ask is not "Would winning or losing the battle be best for the plot or character arc?" but "Is this the right place for the battle?"

If you come to a situation where you simply cannot agree, consider that maybe neither of you is right or wrong —perhaps the material you're looking at is the troublemaker, and moving or removing it would solve the impasse you face with your co-author.

Go back to the roots

When Eileen was doing a work-for-hire project with a publisher, she and the editor bumped heads on the ending. Eileen had agreed to the editor's outline at the start of the project, but in the writing of the story, she gave the character a different motivation from the one the editor had in mind. Since the character and story arrived at the same ending, Eileen didn't think it mattered. Turns out the editor had a strong feeling about motivation.

Rather than resolving this with an arm wrestle or a shouted "My way or I'm out!" they scheduled a time to discuss the core of the story. The editor talked about what inspired the outline she'd created. She talked about issues that were important to her in the story and what the publisher's marketing team were looking forward to selling. Eileen talked about why she felt her motivation made more sense for the particular character.

In the end, they chose to have a secondary character voice the issues the editor and marketing team wanted to include, and Eileen kept the motivation she'd created for the protagonist.

Get a third party's opinion

We're willing to bet that all writers have used a third-party opinion at some point. That's what beta readers are for. They read the manuscript and weigh in with feedback, commenting on what's working and what isn't. If you're traditionally published (or hire an independent editor), the editor acts as a third-party opinion.

If you find that you and your co-author have different ideas about a scene or story direction, you may find it useful to talk to readers about your different ideas.

In co-writing the guides in this series, we typically agree on important decisions, but when we haven't been able to reach a consensus, we've turned to feedback from our beta readers and our mighty editors as the final word on whether something is working or not.

The key to gaining an effective third-party opinion is finding someone who can be impartial. Using your spouse as the third party isn't very fair to the other person because most likely your spouse has a soft spot for you. You also can't set up a discussion with a third party with a statement like "We need you to help us decide the best way to handle this scene—with my innovative creative solution or with Eileen's clunky, cliché-ridden idea."

Look at who has more experience

If you still can't agree, you may have to look at who has more experience in the area of conflict. For instance, if you're the stronger partner on dialogue and you're discussing a dialogue-heavy scene, perhaps you've earned the right to 51% of the vote. But then the percentage flips when it comes to handling version backups since your co-author has more experience with file management.

For areas where you've not assigned a 51% vote, sometimes the person who feels most strongly should hold sway. Creative decisions are rarely a matter of black and white, so unless you're arguing over a decision that has a clear right or wrong—a romance where one partner cheats is a pretty clear wrong in most subgenres, for instance—you have to decide, like in a marriage, if this decision is a hill you want your partnership to die on.

Determine if your conflict is a dealbreaker

You may have tried all the above and discovered that you're still not able to resolve the issue. This doesn't mean that your conflict has to become a huge knock-down fight where you never speak to each other again. But it may be time to look at different ways to write together, or even to dissolve the partnership. We're going to discuss this in more detail in the section How and When Will You End the Partnership?

Your Turn

- Knowing that disagreements will arise, how will you address them?
- What is your conflict style? What is your co-writer's?
- Can you and your co-author agree now to a process for dealing with disagreements, before you're in the heat of a conflict?
- Is there a neutral third party you can turn to when you need another opinion?
- Can you think of any hills you'd be willing to die on—before you're standing on that hill?
- What creative and process areas are you willing to be flexible on?

23

HOW MUCH POLISHING IS ENOUGH?

As we discussed earlier in this book, different authors have different ideas about what "ready for publication" means. And those ideas may depend on which publication route you're going to take.

How will you know you're ready to move on to the publishing phase? What are the cues, or the steps in the process, that will signal you're now in possession of a manuscript that's ready to be unleashed on the world?

Collaborative editing

There is a lot of truth to the saying that all writing is rewriting. We all wish that our first draft was genius, but, alas, it never is. Much like the creation process, editing will require you and your partner to decide what is working and what needs to be changed and polished.

In an ideal world, once you and your co-writer have completed a project, you'll leave it for a week or two so that you can look at it again with fresh eyes. After that period of rest, each co-writer should read the book through, making notes of their thoughts.

You can review the How Will You Write That Book? section and reconsider the options with editing in mind. You may edit collaboratively or relay the edits back and forth. When the Creative Academy team writes these guides, we use a relay style —one person reads the manuscript, polishing and making notes in the margin, and then passes it to the next person. We perform one final read and polish before we pass it to our editor. (Which is when we discover how many typos we overlooked. Raise a glass to the strength of persistent typos.)

If you haven't yet established a file-naming structure for your revisions, now is the time to do that. Seriously. Right now. Do it —before either of you edits a single word and someone's brilliance risks being permanently deleted.

Plan ahead

You can plan ahead and agree on what steps to include in the process. Maybe you're a fan of multiple rounds of edits, including a round with beta readers and another with a developmental editor. Maybe your partner likes to write, pay a proofreader and then fire that book off into the world. One or both of you will need to compromise on your usual approach to saying goodbye to your manuscript.

Since editing often has associated costs, it's especially important to agree to a process at the start of the project.

That said, plans can always be changed. For example, let's say you're a writer who has always hired an editor but, by the time you complete the third round of revisions, you realize that your process has resulted in a much cleaner manuscript than you've ever written on your own. At this stage, you may decide to skip one of your planned editing stages. Removing stages from the process is always easier than adding them in if you've agreed on steps at the start of the project.

Your Turn

Think about what your editing process will look like within your partnership.

- What cues will indicate that your project is done and ready for the next step—publication?
- How many rounds of edits will you commit to?
- Will you have a developmental or substantive edit done?
- Will you have a copy edit done?
- Will you pay for a proofreader?
- Will you rely on beta readers to find typos?
- How will you pay for the costs of the different editing passes?

PART V

HOW WILL YOU HANDLE PUBLICATION?

24

WHAT IS YOUR PUBLICATION GOAL?

You've got a finished manuscript that all writing partners agree is ready to work its way through the publication process and become a real book. You've successfully made it through the creative phase of the project, and you're still friends (or at the very least professionals). You're excited to take things to the next level, get this story into the hands of readers and turn this book into a revenue-generating machine.

Now it's time to go back, look at the goals you set for yourselves and determine if those publication goals have changed or shifted.

Remind yourselves of the outcome, process and performance goals you set when you started writing together. Over the course of a multi-month project, we can lose track of our why and how or even change our minds. There are many good reasons to pivot at this stage. For instance, if your original plan was to co-author a book to pitch to a publisher but current events suggest your book would be timely if it came out now, you might adjust your publication goal—traditional publication can take one to three years.

At this juncture, sit down with your co-author and consider the following question:

> Right now, what do I want the results of publishing this book to be?

Are you looking to add to your monthly income? Establish yourself in a new genre in which your co-author is already rocking it? Break into traditional publishing with the help of your partner's connections?

Are you trying to hit a bestseller list or expand your audience? Or maybe you wrote with your friends just for fun and look forward to helping each other cross-promote this one book.

It's important to revisit and recommit to your publishing goal now because each one lends itself to a different possible path to publication, as well as different business models.

Your Turn

Review the goals you set and discussed with your partner in the What Is Your Author Goal? section of this book.

- Has anything changed?
- If so, what is your new agreed-upon publication plan?

25

WHAT IS YOUR PUBLICATION PATH?

Hopefully in the pre-writing stage of developing your co-author partnership you discussed and agreed on a publication path, whether your plan was to indie publish or seek an agent to help you traditionally publish.

If you're reading through this book before making publication decisions or wooing a co-author, this section might help you decide which approach will best serve your broader author goals.

Indie publishing

Indie publishing is also referred to as self-publishing. We prefer the term *indie publishing* to clarify that while you are responsible for the entire publishing process, you may choose to contract out different aspects of the business, such as editing, cover design and layout. There are usually costs related to contracting for these services, but with indie publishing you maintain total control of who you work with and the direction of your project.

If you and your co-author have decided to indie publish, the 101 tasks you need to complete should have been at least broadly divvied up by this stage. If they haven't, this would be a perfect time for you and your co-author to settle in with a nice pot of tea or bottle of wine and make a detailed list of who'll do what.

If you're not sure of the tasks required to get from holding a publish-ready manuscript to holding an e-reader with your title on it, take a trip over to the CreativeAcademyForWriters.com community. We have weekly office hours and dozens of recorded and live resources to help you with this stage of your author career.

Traditional publishing

Traditional publishing means that you and your co-writer will seek an established publishing house to license the rights to your book and distribute it to readers. In this model, the publishing house is responsible for the 101 tasks, including editorial notes on your manuscript (which will mean another round of editing), cover design, book layout, the provision of your book to retailers, and so on. As an author, you do not pay for any of these services up front, but you do pay in the form of the royalty share that the publisher keeps for each sale of your book.

As an outcome goal, traditional publication is something you, as the author, have little control over. Certainly you control whether to seek an agent to represent your book to the big publishing houses, but you can't control whether you'll actually find an agent willing to take your project. You can control your outreach to smaller publishers that accept author submissions, but not whether your book will be offered a publication contract.

Given how much is out of your control in traditional publishing, you and your co-author would do well to set some deadlines for results.

- How many months will you work on finding an agent?

- Alternately, how many rejections will trigger a move to a different approach, such as seeking publication with a small publisher?
- How many small publishers will you approach?
- How many rejections will trigger a move to a different approach, such as indie publishing?

The sections that follow will help you answer many different questions and formulate a clearer picture of the kind of publishing relationship you want to have with your co-authors.

We can't include *everything* about traditional and indie publishing in this book, so we've focused on the areas and decisions that are critical to publishing with co-authors.

But, depending on your broader author business goals, other books in this series would be good additional reading.

If you're looking for a more in-depth discussion about indie and traditional publishing, including the pros and cons of each, *Full Time Author* covers this in detail.

If indie publishing feels right for you, you'll likely want to read *Strategic Indie Author* to help you develop your specific strategic approach.

If co-authoring has lit a fire that makes you want to write more books in a shared world, *Strategic Series Author* is the guide for you.

Your Turn

Consider your gut response to the two models of publishing.

- What aspects of indie publishing appeal to you?

- What parts of indie publishing make you uncomfortable?
- What aspects of traditional publishing appeal to you?
- What parts of traditional publishing make you uncomfortable?
- How does your co-author feel about the options? Are there some options that are off the table for the person or yourself?
- Do you and your co-authors share a preference for a specific publishing path?
- What specific skills and resources do you bring to each model of publishing?
- What specific skills and resources does your co-writer bring to each model?
- Can your discomfort with one method be alleviated by your co-author's comfort, confidence or experience in that area, or vice versa?
- Is the publishing model you prefer a hill you're willing to die on? If so, why? (Is it due to contract limits you have with an existing agent or publisher? Is it based on the anticipated expenses? Is it a control issue?)
- What publishing path have you and your co-author(s) chosen?

26
WHAT FORM WILL YOUR SHARED PUBLISHING BUSINESS TAKE?

From a casual handshake agreement to co-write one novella to plans for a ten-part series, the way you structure your co-author business will depend on a number of factors. While there is no right or wrong business model, some models are better suited to certain types of author relationships.

And, as warm and fuzzy as a handshake agreement feels, it's always good form to write down expectations in at least a semi-legal document. Co-authors can refer to it when a decision from months earlier becomes a point of confusion or, worse, conflict.

At the end of this section, the Your Turn activity will help you identify questions you might like to discuss as you consider options for your co-author business arrangement.

The more simple and straightforward you keep your business structure and systems, the less time you'll need to spend on the management of the partnership. Less time spent on administrative details means more time for writing and marketing those great books you're going to create.

But while simple can be good, it's important to be aware of "simple solutions" that have long-term implications. For instance, the decision about who registers a copyright and purchases ISBNs for shared books will have ramifications for the life of the books. The simple solution is not always the best solution for the long term.

We can't predict everything, and sometimes projects take on a life of their own, growing in unexpected and fantastic ways. If you do end up in a situation where something core to your author partnership needs to be adjusted at a later date, know you're in good company.

It's unlikely you'll be the first co-author team facing that sticky situation—good sticky like toffee pudding, or bad sticky like gum in your hair—and writing communities are a great place to gather information before you consult the appropriate expert (accountant, business advisor, publishing industry professional or lawyer) to outline your options and explain consequences of each of the choices available to you.

What follows are a number of common co-author business scenarios to consider and discuss.

We've expressed them in terms of romantic relationships to help you appreciate the level of commitment required for each. And remember, just like in the dating world, you can always start as casual partners and build toward a more permanent relationship as you write and publish stories readers love.

Casual hookup = contributing to an anthology or boxed set

If a group of authors is interested in writing stories with a specific theme or shared premise, then you've got the highest level of flexibility and the lowest commitment possible.

- Each author writes their story and submits it to the anthology organizer.

- Each author pays for their own editing.
- There is often a small buy-in to pay for the anthology book cover.
- Most often, these books sell for $0.99, so although royalties are collected, they will rarely add up to more than $100 per author—which is why so many anthologies donate their proceeds to charity.
- Each author maintains the copyright to the characters and settings in the world they write.
- As a group, you decide if the book will be published wide or in Kindle Unlimited.
- As a group, you decide how long you'll maintain your book in the anthology. This is typically three to six months. At the end of the commitment period, the anthology is taken out of publication and each author can use their story for whatever they want—as a free book to attract newsletter sign-ups, a prequel to a new series, bonus content in an existing series… The savvy author will have a strategic purpose in mind for their anthology contribution before they write it.
- The biggest commitment in this scenario relates to cross-promoting the box set or anthology. That is where the real value in this kind of co-author relationship exists, and it's where you can make or break future co-author relationships. Authors who join groups like this and don't pull their weight by supporting the co-authored book find it hard to be accepted into new co-authored worlds and series.

Dating = writing in an indie author's established shared-world series

This level of co-author relationship requires being in touch regularly to keep abreast of what's happening in the world and with the series in progress.

- Each author publishes their own book under their name.
- Each author pays for their own editing.
- One person will likely design all the book covers in the series while each author pays an agreed-upon design fee for their cover.
- Each author keeps all royalties received from sales of their own book.
- Copyright to an author's new characters and settings in the world can vary by series. This is an important point to review.
- The series owner decides whether the series will be published wide or in Kindle Unlimited.
- The series owner will let contributing authors know how long they must keep their books in the series.
- As with the casual hookup, the biggest commitment relates to cross-promoting each other's titles. Shared-world authors rely on readers moving from one book in the series to another, so promoting your co-authors' books is required and has the benefit of supporting all authors in the series. Authors who join groups like this and don't promote each other's titles won't get invited back to subsequent series in the world.

Living together = co-writing shared books

Writing together and living together are similar in so many ways. You're committed, but there's still a chance to walk away. Also, when you first move in together—into a shared word processing document, that is—there can be more questions than answers. The rules of the relationship are broad and basically up to you and your co-author.

- You can each have your name on book covers and copyright documents, or you can pick a pen name.
- As a team, you decide all costs related to the editing stage of your manuscript.

- As a team, you agree on a book cover. If you're lucky, one of you has design skills. If not, the cost of the design will need to be negotiated. Professional covers can cost anywhere from $50 to more than $500.
- As a team, you determine how to set up royalty sharing. The distribution of royalties can be handled by publishing software if you're willing to pay for it.
- Copyright to the characters and settings in the world will technically belong to both of you unless you state otherwise in a contract.
- Whether you publish wide or in Kindle Unlimited is a business decision you'll make together.
- How long you'll keep your co-author titles available is another joint decision. But know that once a book is published, places like Goodreads will maintain the details about it forever, even if you take it out of print. So if you have any concerns about featuring your name on a book with your co-author, or if you think that one day in a distant future the relationship might come back to bite you, be aware of the legacy of your co-authored work.
- How best to market and promote your book is a decision you'll make together. (In a world where unicorns dance on rainbows, you'd hire a marketing company to do this work for you.)

Marriage = writing for a publisher's established shared-world series

This level of co-author relationship requires you to give up more creative freedom than most other co-author relationships.

- Each author's book is published under their own author name.
- The publisher assigns each author an editor and pays the costs.
- The editor may have final say on many things related to

the story—length, types of characters, plot lines, settings and so on.
- Traditional publishers generally handle the book cover, while small indie publishers may allow the author to take care of that—at their own expense, of course.
- The publisher manages the royalties and pays the author their share.
- Copyright in core characters and settings belongs to the publisher. Copyright in characters and settings brought to the world by contributing authors needs to be negotiated. This is an important point to discuss.
- The series owner decides in which markets the books are published and at what price point.
- The series owner tells contributing authors how long they must keep their books in the series. This will be in the contract.
- Some publishers require their authors to do promotion, which can vary widely, from a few social media posts a month to participating in blog hops, joining promo groups, and supporting the book launches of other authors in the series. The contract will make these commitments clear.

Marriage + kids = setting up your own shared publishing company

Like kids, your books will be around for a long time, and setting up a publishing company with your co-authors means entering into a relationship that will last the lifetime of your creative works and potentially outlive you. Like when raising kids, you have to be flexible, figure out what works for you along the way, and decide at each stage of business development how you'll move forward.

Look at the previous section to get a sense of the decisions you'll need to make. In the sections that follow, we walk you through some options for dealing with these decisions in key areas of your publishing business.

A note on polyamorous writing relationships

There are no limits on the number of co-authors you can write with. But remember—each person you add to the mix makes it exponentially more complex to manage the book, because everyone comes to the table with their own ideas, history and experiences. On the upside and downside, when you play the what-if game at the planning stage, there are that many more brains in the mix.

We totally support multi-author collaborations—hey, there are three of us in the Creative Academy Guides for Writers team—as long as you go into it understanding that more authors increases the necessity of maintaining good communication, good organization and regular check-ins to make sure everything is running smoothly and everyone is being heard. Don't worry, we've got a whole section on that coming up.

How are decisions made?

It's important to have a process in place for making decisions within your publishing business. It may be an equal power relationship, or there may be dynamics at work that give one of the partners more votes, or more of a say than others in certain areas. Make sure you clearly understand the existing power structure and what that means for you in terms of the business going forward.

Before you start publishing (or sign anything)

No matter what structure your shared writing business will have, it's extremely important to agree on your intended publication path and how to run your shared publishing business before you actually publish the books—and ideally before you even write them. This way, if there are any issues, you can work them out before contracts have been signed and before there is money on (or off!) the table.

In the sections that follow, we share as many questions as we do answers. But working through those questions with your partners is exactly what you need to do to clarify all aspects of your business arrangements.

Your Turn

- How comfortable are you with the idea of a collaborative business relationship?
- How confident are you that this partnership will be long-term?
- How confident are you that this partnership project will be profitable?
- Can your collaborative projects work within the context of your existing author businesses?
- Is there a practical or legal reason to create a separate legal entity for your co-authored projects?
- Do you have author colleagues who are willing to share sample contracts they've signed with co-authors?
- Have any partners already set up an established publishing business? What are the benefits to using that established business for this shared project? What are the drawbacks?

(Author's note: If your co-writing preference is to keep it light and casual, then move on to the next section of the book.)

If you believe that your partnership will be long-term or profitable enough to benefit from a shared publishing business, work through the following questions with your potential business partners, and pay particular attention to the contracts section that follows.

- Which elements of your publishing business actually *need* to be shared?
- Have any of the partners run their own business before? What went well? What didn't? What was learned from that experience?
- What skills or experience do you or your co-author(s) have that are relevant to running a publishing business?
- Does anyone in your partnership want to assume control of the management of a shared author business? If not, are you willing to pay a bookkeeper and others to handle admin tasks?
- Are you and your co-authors based in the same country? If not, this can create interesting (read challenging) taxation situations.
- Does anyone have a financial or relationship history that might impact your shared business activities? (Examples include a divorce in progress, bad credit history, a criminal conviction.)

27

WHAT CONTRACTS DO YOU NEED IN PLACE BEFORE YOU GET STARTED?

Different writing partnerships require different kinds of paperwork.

Regardless of how formal your documentation is—whether or not a lawyer is involved in drawing it up—putting things on paper forces you to spell out the exact terms of your working partnership, and ensures that everyone agrees to those terms before your relationship is formalized.

Asking questions helps guide you through important discussions and decisions, ensuring you and your co-author share a vision about what you're doing and how your relationship will function. It is far more enjoyable to work out these problems at the start than to figure them out in the middle of a stressful decision.

This is where we remind you that we are not lawyers.

Sure, we may write characters who are lawyers, and we might throw around fancy legal vocabulary, but that's not even close to the same thing.

Rules about legal documentation vary widely depending on your geographic location and that of your partners. What follows is definitely *not* legal advice and should not be considered as such. The sample questions and suggestions we share here are only to help you get the conversation started, and to give you some idea of the questions you'll need to answer in order to get actual legal documents drawn up. Years of watching *The People's Court* and reading legal thrillers has in no way qualified us to give you legal advice.

If you can't afford professional legal help, you can check out the resources offered by the Alliance of Independent Authors, which has template contracts available to members. At the time of writing, those documents do include a sample working agreement for co-authors as well as a publication contract for co-authors. They also have lawyers who answer member questions.

Various writing organizations or writer's unions may also provide legal support services.

Questions to ask before signing a publishing or co-author agreement:

- What rights (formats, territories) are being licensed?
- Are those rights exclusive, or can you publish the stories in other places or formats?
- How do you get your rights back? Are you licensing the rights for a certain time period? Or until sales drop below a certain threshold? Or something else?
- What sub-rights will you retain? The rights to sell into foreign markets? Translations? Audiobooks? Merchandise featuring your characters?
- Who owns the world that you're writing in? Which parts of the world are yours and which aren't?
- Will you be allowed to write future books, outside of the shared world, with the characters you create?
- Is there anything in the contract that will restrict your future author opportunities?

Our Creative Academy team meets for a full day every 12 weeks to review where our business is at and talk about where we're headed. When it came time to document our partnership, we spent several sessions working through the different types of agreements we needed to put together, playing the what-if game until we were confident we had considered every good, bad, ugly and impossible situation. We asked friends and spouses to help us brainstorm scenarios they thought could break us up, and then we brainstormed solutions and workarounds.

There may have been wine. There were definitely tears. Nobody likes to consider the prospect of one of the partners dying, but when copyright and dollar bills and legacies are at play, that's the level of discussion that needs to happen.

Working agreements

At the very least, every co-author partnership should have a working agreement in place before writing starts. Even if it's an informal one, just the process of deciding who will be responsible for what, and by when, will help keep your partnership running smoothly.

Key components of a working agreement

- Co-author legal names and full mailing addresses
- Estimated length, working title and genre of the book
- Description of the type of legal business partnership (if any) that exists
- Name of the copyright holder
- Author names that will appear on the cover
- Description of how expenses for the project will be handled
- Description of how royalties will be broken up (% to each author), including details for each format you will or could publish

- Description of how tasks will be divided between co-authors, ideally through all phases of the project (research, writing, editing, formatting, publishing and promotion)
- Description of what happens if a partner cannot or will not complete the work they have agreed to do
- Description of how you will resolve conflicts if you cannot come to an agreement

Strong working agreements also generally include several other "legalese"-type clauses that cover what happens if someone dies, what happens when dealing with agents or other parties, and anything else that may be specific to your country's laws, the subject of your book, or your personal situation.

Even if you use a lawyer-approved template to generate a working agreement, it's always a good idea to have a lawyer review your specific contracts.

Publication agreements

If you are going the traditional publishing route with your books, then it'll be up to your publisher to provide you (and your co-authors) with a publication agreement. This will include things such as royalty rates, specific rights to be licensed, bonus clauses and option clauses. You, or your agent if you have one, will need to inform the publisher of your co-author status on the project when you submit it, and you can work out with them how royalties are to be paid out. The publisher will defer to the agreement made by the authors. If you state it is to be a 50-50 split, then that is how they will do it. If you've already agreed on a 60-40 split, that is how it will be divided.

If you're indie publishing, you must ensure your co-authoring agreement covers all of these important details.

If you're forming an independent publishing company as a partnership, or an incorporated company that is a separate entity from you as individuals, you can consider signing a publishing agreement to license your work to your shared company.

This type of publication agreement needs to address all the same questions and issues that a publishing house's contract would. We are definitely getting into "consult professionals" territory here, but if you'd like to put together your own contract before approaching a lawyer to review it, consider purchasing the Contracts Self-Help Package from the Writers' Union of Canada. It includes a Model Trade Book Contract (updated in 2021) as well as a guide on what questions to ask and what to watch for.

Many other sample publishing contracts are available online. Make sure you're reviewing one from a reputable source that has the interests of the authors at heart.

Partnership agreements and incorporation documents

If you're registering your publishing business as a legal partnership or corporation, the specific documents you need to complete and file will vary by country and by state or province. That paperwork will address many of the questions in the following sections. Business registration is also required to conduct activities such as creating a joint bank account in the name of your partnership, opening a separate publishing account for your partnership and creating an ISBN account owned by your partnership.

If you're thinking, *Holy moly, that sounds like a lot of extra work and expense*, you're not wrong. It is. But the short-term inconvenience will reap several long-term benefits for partnerships that expect to publish several titles together:

- Potential tax advantages
- Protection for partners should legal issues arise from any of your co-published books
- Assurance that shared assets stay shared assets

- Assurance that intellectual property will remain intact in the event that something terrible happens to one of the partners

At the very least, we at the Creative Academy found that the process of creating a formalized partnership agreement forced us to figure out in advance how we'd handle all kinds of what-if scenarios, including fun topics like what would happen if Eileen got hit by a bus.

If issues arise down the road, we have not only a road map to deal with it, but also a written acknowledgement by all parties that shows very clearly what we agreed to. This way any heirs or executors will know what the person wanted (other than to miss being hit by that bus).

As with co-author and publishing agreements, you can find partnership agreement templates online to give you a solid starting place.

Key elements in a partnership agreement

- Legal names and legal addresses of the partners
- Name of the partnership
- Purpose of the partnership
- Term of the partnership
- Place of business
- Capital contributions each partner is making
- Information about which capital accounts the partnership will hold
- Guidelines for making financial decisions
- Each partner's ownership interest in the partnership
- Breakdown of profit and loss sharing
- Tax procedures
- Votes per partner
- Accounting procedures
- Annual reporting requirements
- Dates for the partnership's fiscal year

- When and how the partnership will internally audit its finances
- Description of how the partnership will be managed
- Compensation, if any, for services rendered by partners
- Personnel in charge of filing annual tax returns
- Schedule and location of partnership meetings
- Procedure for admittance of new partners
- Procedure for leaving the partnership (voluntarily)
- Procedure for removing a partner from the partnership
- Procedure for dissolving the partnership
- Various legalese-type clauses around liability, insurance and governing laws or jurisdictions that apply to the agreement
- Dates and signatures of all parties

When to get professional advice

It's always best to have an agent or intellectual property attorney review any and all contracts you are given.

And always read every word on every page of every contract you sign. If there is anything you don't understand, you have questions about, or that makes you feel uncomfortable (even if you don't know why), consult a professional.

When in doubt, ask questions. This is your career—you should understand it.

Your Turn

- Do you have a working agreement in place with your co-authors?
- Play the what-if game. What if something happens to a partner?

- What if your co-authored book becomes a runaway bestseller?
- What if one partner wants to keep writing in your shared world and the other is happy to stop at one story?
- Who will take responsibility for finding an agreement template or hiring a professional to write an agreement for you?
- How much are you willing to invest in creating a legal agreement? Who will pay the fees associated with that?

28

HOW WILL YOU SELL THE BOOKS?

This isn't an exhaustive discussion of what's involved in traditional or indie publishing. If you're looking for something to walk you through step by step, check out *Full Time Author* for its in-depth discussion of traditional and indie publishing. *Strategic Indie Author* covers the indie publishing process in greater detail and guides you through exactly what strategies and tools will be a good fit for you. Below, we've highlighted questions to help you and your partners choose the path that's the best match for your team.

Selling to a publisher

Financially and structurally, selling your book to a publisher is the most straightforward option.

The publisher will license rights to sell your book, typically in both print and eBook formats, for a set territory (such as World, North America, UK). The publisher will take responsibility for printing and production costs and provide sales venues (stores, online retailers) with copies of your book.

The publisher will track sales numbers and finances and will issue you royalty cheques. Typically, publishers pay royalties twice a year, although you may have also received an advance payment. You don't have to manage any of the practical requirements for actually selling the books, beyond helping the publisher drive customers toward places they can be purchased. (Do you like how we made this last bit sound easy?)

Selling via distributors and aggregators

If you're indie publishing, you can use aggregators or distributors to handle most of the actual selling to customers. Companies like Draft2Digital, PublishDrive, IngramSpark, PubShare and many others will let you upload your book files to their sites. They will then publish your book on various storefronts, collect the revenues and pay your royalties each month. Some take a monthly fee (PublishDrive), some keep a percentage of your royalties (Draft2Digital and PubShare), and some charge a fee when you upload your book as well as an annual catalogue fee (IngramSpark).

In all these cases, the bookstores make your books available for sale, and it's your job to drive customers to them.

The benefits of using an aggregator or distributor as a co-author team is that royalties can be divided at the source, and the company will send each author their share. We've heard horror stories from a small number of co-authors who've had the bad experience of giving royalty-payment responsibility to someone who accepted the sales revenue but never transferred a dollar to the co-authors. Sadly, the legal costs involved in chasing down a shady player like this is often not worth the payout.

Consider the following questions. While you're brainstorming, we highly recommend you play the what-if game to future-test every decision you make.

- What publishing account will you use? One of the partner's existing accounts? A new shared account?
- If you use an existing partner's account, what systems are in place to keep the information about your shared books separate from that author's personal book revenues?
- How will the partner who is not on the account access information? Be aware that royalties will be paid in combined payments to the existing bank account unless you create a new account.
- Who will take care of the paperwork?

Selling via online bookstores

Many online bookstores—Kobo, Apple Books, Google Play, Amazon, Nook (Barnes & Noble)—will let you create accounts and upload books directly.

Some bookstores, however, don't allow direct uploading. In those cases, you need to go through an aggregator or distributor.

In either case, the bookstores make the books available to purchase, and it's your job to drive customers to them.

Selling direct to readers

If you're going to sell direct to readers, things get more complicated.

eBooks

If you're selling eBooks direct to readers, you can use software like Shopify, Payhip, Gumroad or PayPal to collect money from customers. You can manually deliver the eBook files to your customers or use software to auto-deliver your products. You may need to use a service like BookFunnel in combination with a payment processor to deliver your digital products. While each platform works a bit differently, make sure to process payments securely, collect the correct taxes and submit them to the proper regionally specific authorities. You will also have to handle support for your customers.

Print books

You can use the same method for collecting money for print books as eBooks if you have the stock on hand, or you can use print-on-demand technology to ship the book direct to your customer from IngramSpark or KDP Print.

The challenge? With print books, you're dealing with shipping on top of everything else. There are a lot of questions you'll need to answer, and we've included many below. As always in a co-author situation, you need to make sure everyone's on the same page.

Consider the following questions. While you're brainstorming, we highly recommend you play the what-if game to future-test every decision you make.

- Who will handle obtaining, storing and shipping inventory?
- How will you handle fulfilling orders?
- Who will pay the shipping?
- Who will handle payment processing, and what tool or company will you use?
- How will you manage sales taxes?
- How will you handle the upgraded security required on your website if you're processing credit card information?
- Do co-authors get to buy books at cost if they're going to resell them?
- Are there rules around direct-sales pricing at events?
- Are there rules around who can sell at which events?
- Who will calculate expenses and revenue payouts?
- Will you allow returns? What is your returns policy?
- Who will handle returns and how?

- How will you account for returns in your bookkeeping and payout process?
- Who will provide tech support to your customers?

Your Turn

- Go to the corresponding section in the *Create With Co-Authors* workbook Google Doc, discuss the questions with your co-authors, then fill in your answers as you agree on things.
- Which of these options for selling your books will your co-author business employ?
- If you are indie publishing, which formats (eBooks, print books, audiobooks) will you produce?

29

HOW ARE REVENUES SHARED?

The question of revenue sharing seems simple, and in some cases the answer *is* simple. For example, co-authors writing in a shared world but publishing from their own accounts may agree that everyone keeps the revenue generated by their own books.

And, in a situation where multiple authors contribute to an eBook anthology or digitally published boxed set, everyone might agree to split royalties equally. The math would be pretty straightforward, and there are a variety of tools available to distribute the funds. Figuring out publication costs and responsibilities (like designing the book cover and project management) can add some extra figuring, but typically it's not too complex.

But let's have a look at a model that isn't so straightforward—the one we use to share royalties from The Creative Academy Guides for Writers.

Case Study: The Creative Academy Guides for Writers

The model for our Creative Academy publishing company is both logical and flexible, although somewhat complex in its breakdown now that we've been growing the business and expanding our options over a period of years. But the basic logic remains consistent.

Books with three authors contributing equally:

- 10% of royalties are paid to the "house"—our joint business bank account
- 30% of royalties are paid to each of the three of us *after* our shared expenses are deducted
- Shared expenses include things like hiring an editor, paying for ads, paying our ad manager and paying for PublishDrive

Books with two authors contributing equally:

- 10% of royalties are paid to the "house"
- 45% of royalties are paid to each author after shared expenses are paid
- Both authors share expenses like hiring an editor, cover design and the cost of publication assistance
- 10% of advertising costs are paid by the "house" because ads also benefit other books in the series

Books with a single author:

- 10% of royalties are paid to the "house"
- 90% of royalties are paid to the author
- 100% of editing and publication expenses are paid by the author
- 10% of advertising costs are paid by the "house" because ads also benefit other books in the series

For revenue generated from other sources such as affiliates and subsidiary rights, we have agreed on similar percentages. Make sure to detail arrangements for this other income in your publication contracts and business agreements.

So far, so good. Having an agreement about who gets what—and who pays for what—is fabulous. Now you need a system for receiving and disbursing those funds to co-authors.

Dealing with royalties

Unlike the olden days, when calculating royalty splits on co-authored books was a royal(ty) pain in the behind that required some serious ninja spreadsheet skills, managing the books today is simply a matter of deciding which tool to use. The best tool for the job depends on your budget and which distributor you're using for your books.

Getting paid by your publisher

If you're working with a traditional publisher for your co-authored book, your publisher will generally pay you out individually. However, if your writing partnership is set up as its own entity—an incorporated company or limited liability partnership—then the publisher or agent may pay out the business. It would be up to you to divvy up the income according to the terms of the contract with your co-author.

If you are indie publishing your collaborative works, you have a few possible setups and tools to help you manage royalty payments.

Maintaining separate publishing accounts

If your co-author arrangement has you publishing your own books through your own publishing accounts, you can just check this box and move on—using your existing accounts should work just fine.

Using one partner's publishing accounts

It's possible for one partner to handle publishing and accounting for royalties for all the partners, while you publish the books from that partner's publishing account. But we recommend you think hard before committing to this approach.

Why? Because each month, someone will have to manually calculate payouts and figure out which revenue belongs to shared books and which doesn't. In addition, this approach can cause complications at tax time since the revenue documents provided by online bookstores will not itemize the income sources separately. Net result? A big job to track and handle the required paperwork, and added risk for any partner whose name is not on the account.

Sharing publishing accounts on various stores

You can set up a separate account under the managing partner's name or under a shared pen name, then split the revenue according to your publication agreement. Once a month, the money will come into the appointed bank account, and you will pay out partners on your established schedule.

If you choose this option, your internal documentation will become even more important, especially if any online bookstores require you to verify your copyright or ownership of the book materials in the account.

Putting publishing accounts in the name of your shared business

If you register your partnership as an official business, you'll be able to open bank accounts in the name of your business and automatically set up and connect publishing accounts to that business. The owners of record for that business will be documented in your incorporation or partnership documents. You'll get tax documentation from each company that sells your books, and you will either file taxes as your business, or claim your income from this business when you file your individual taxes.

Our advice? Speak with your accountant about what makes the most sense and what level of financial tracking your government requires.

Using a publishing platform with built-in splitting tools

It's an exciting time for co-authorship because several companies have royalty-splitting options built right into their publishing platforms. This offers the best of both worlds—you can easily set up payment splitting with only a casual level of oversight, and you can keep your focus on the writing. This means you don't have to establish a whole separate business to collaborate with other authors. For writers looking to avoid a marriage-level commitment, this is what you've been waiting for!

Below, we outline a few leaders in this area (at the time of writing). Ask your writing communities about their experiences with these companies, or do some research online to make sure you find the best fit for your needs.

There may be other options that we haven't listed here, including those that specialize in your geographic region or specific genre.

Draft2Digital

Draft2Digital has a royalty-splitting option that can be used in a variety of ways for different kinds of co-authored projects. Some highlights of the Draft2Digital platform include:

- The ability for one organizer to set up the project and invite their collaborators to join
- The ability to assign different percentage splits to different contributing authors, with D2D paying out collaborators each month for their share of the revenue (in this case, each collaborator must create a D2D account and fill out their individual tax interview)

Draft2Digital is a great option if you've got collaborators in different countries, or you want to do collaborative projects without combining your businesses or publishing accounts in any other way.

At the time of writing, Draft2Digital keeps 10% of all revenues from the sales of your projects. There is no monthly fee and no risk for you. But be aware that there's no cap on the fees, which means if you have revenues of $10,000 a month, you'll be paying one thousand of those dollars to D2D.

The good news? You'll only pay fees if you're making money.

PubShare (formerly BundleRabbit)

PubShare operates similarly to Draft2Digital in many ways. PubShare keeps 10% of revenues from all projects so you only pay fees if you're making money. They pay out authors each month via PayPal. And you can publish and distribute paperbacks, eBooks, and hardcovers through their platform. They also have some interesting shared-world functionality—so if you're setting up a shared-world series in which various authors write, check out this option.

PublishDrive

PublishDrive offers two options for splitting royalties: Team Royalties and Abacus. Each have set fees, so they are most beneficial for authors who are earning stable or increasing royalties with their shared products. The service fees don't change, so the more you make from your book sales, the more you "save" by choosing PublishDrive.

Team Royalties is a function that lets you distribute your book through PublishDrive. For a per-book, per-author, per-month fee, they collect, calculate, and pay out each author according to the percentages you specify when you set up the book.

Abacus is their other option. This is for books that are *not* published through PublishDrive, such as books published direct to Amazon via KDP. You can upload your Amazon sales reports (and manually add revenue and expenses from other platforms) to Abacus and, for a set fee per product per month, the platform calculates how much is owed to each author.

Payouts happen manually, not automatically, so someone on your team must enter data and pay out each author according to the information.

Using multiple currencies

While we all like money and are happy to take it from any and all countries, dealing with income in multiple currencies—not to mention various sales platforms and partners who are not located in the same country—will require some planning.

Make sure the primary currency for payouts will work for all co-authors favourably when it comes to exchange rates. Some banks charge service fees to receive foreign currency, so make sure your choice minimizes those fees.

Payout considerations

Do all of your partners have access to the banking system that's needed to receive their payouts? Some countries, for example, don't have PayPal or Stripe. Some can't receive bank transfers from US companies. It's important to make sure everyone in your co-author team has a way to receive their royalty share.

Your Turn

Work your way through the questions below. Make sure your working agreement or publishing contract answers these questions, and that all co-authors agree on the answers.

- What percentage of royalties and revenue will each partner get?
- What potential expenses have you agreed upon? Think about agent percentage, costs for advertising, swag for conferences, free copies for reviewers.
- Are potential expenses different for different formats of the book?
- What rights are included in your shared publication agreement?
- Is the royalty rate the same for each book or story within an anthology, boxed set or series?
- How is that tracked and calculated?
- Who handles royalty tracking and calculations?
- Who handles payouts?
- Does a co-author receive extra compensation for handling admin tasks?
- Are there extra expenses for tools to handle admin tasks?
- What is the payout schedule? Remember that while you will pay expenses in real time, you will receive royalties from most platforms 30 to 90 days after the sales are made.
- What is your primary currency?
- Are there limitations on how you and your partners can receive money?
- What process will you put in place in case something happens to the person managing the money?
- Are you using shared publishing or bank accounts?
- If you are using shared accounts, do all partners have access to those accounts? How is that managed?
- What official paperwork needs to be created, shared or stored?

30

HOW WILL YOU HANDLE TAXES?

It is said that only two things are inevitable: death and taxes. And if you don't want to die from stress-related causes, you need a plan to address your publishing tax responsibilities.

There are several contexts where taxes are relevant to your writing business and where you need to stay on top of things no matter what kind of co-authoring arrangement you have. Despite the amount of time we spend dealing with this stuff, we're not accountants (although Crystal has learned enough that if this authoring thing doesn't work out, she's going back to school for accounting. That woman gets *waaaay* too excited about spreadsheets).

We're all Canadian (although Eileen is a dual citizen because she's special), so our experience should be taken as a guide, not advice—other than to do your research and find out what's required in your country for the specific type of business partnership you've chosen. This is one of those times when it pays to gather up all your questions and spend an hour with a professional, getting the answers you need.

Paying income taxes

Guess what—if you're making money from your writing, you need to track that stream of moolah rolling into your bank account and declare it to the government. You can be sure that the companies transferring royalty funds to you are reporting that on their spreadsheets.

Develop a system to track your income. Download data from your publishing accounts each year before providing your paperwork to your accountant. Also download all the official company forms that summarize your income from the year. This will help you file accurate tax returns and minimize the odds of suffering the pain of a tax audit.

Collecting sales tax

Most authors these days sell the majority of their books through a distributor or aggregator. Those online bookstores and physical distributors should be collecting the appropriate sales tax from the people who purchase your books. Be sure to read the updates, notices and disclaimers you receive from your booksellers since things can and do change from time to time.

If you move and change countries, you must update your address in your publishing accounts. This will help ensure the paperwork you get from the booksellers—and thus your income and tax filing information—is accurate.

Registering for "optional" taxes

There are some taxes that your business may or may not need to track and pay. In Canada, we have Goods and Services Tax (GST), for which your business doesn't have to register until you hit a certain level of income. You can register before that if you want. (It's a bit complicated, but sometimes the extra tracking and reporting is worth it because you might receive money back from the government if you're paying more than you collect.) It's up to the individual or business to realize that they have hit that threshold and then register.

Paying your business or income taxes

If you have chosen to have a "marriage" type of business partnership that's registered with the government, you'll need to find out what kind of income taxes and documentation you are required to file, and what you need to track throughout the year in order to do your due diligence come tax time.

Tools to use for business bookkeeping

When considering which tools you'll use to track income and expenses, track taxes collected and paid out, and generally track your business bookkeeping for your co-author partnership, keep in mind that your tools need to be sustainable both while you're using them and, if necessary, after the partnership wraps up.

At The Creative Academy, for example, we used to use simple spreadsheets to track our income and expenses, which was fine for the way our partnership was set up at the time.

But once we had to register for GST and start filing income taxes as a registered partnership, we needed to get a bit more official with the bookkeeping. While Donna and Eileen were having a panic attack, Crystal was giddy about all the options (one of the benefits of having partners!). When choosing accounting software, there are many good options available—and some of them are cloud-based, which makes it easy for all partners to enter and retrieve information as needed.

If you're using a cloud-based service, make sure the software has the capacity to export all your business records and archive them somewhere outside the paid service. If it doesn't, you'll need to set aside enough money to cover the cost of that tool until you close out your partnership's finances.

Where we live, business records must be maintained for seven years, even after a business is closed. When we were trying to decide between the convenience of cloud-based accounting software and the price and capabilities of the desktop version, it became clear that the seven-year requirement would cost us thousands of dollars for years *after* we needed it if we committed to cloud-based software. That made our choice simple.

Your Turn

Speak to your accountant about your co-author plans and the impact they may have on your business income and expense tracking.

- Do your accountant have the experience to work with your file given the new parameters?
- If not, can they suggest an accountant who works with authors specifically?
- If they don't have a recommendation, ask your author community for recommendations.
- Also ask your author community what snafus they've faced so you have questions to ask any new accountant.
- Schedule an introductory call with potential new accountants to gauge their experience dealing with the quirks of a writing and publishing business.
- Do you have a system to organize your income documentation through the year?
- Who within your partnership will be responsible for keeping your records up to date?
- Have you filled out the tax interview documentation on each of the publisher, distributor and aggregator platforms you use?
- What software or tools will you use to track income and expenses for your business?

- Are you doing any direct selling of books?
- If yes, how will you collect sales tax? Will it be added to the cover price at point of purchase, or blended in? How will you track the sales tax you've collected? Who will submit sales tax to the appropriate authorities?
- Are there taxes in your country, state or province that you may need to collect and submit? Is there a threshold for collecting those taxes? Has your author business met that threshold? If not, review your sales at regular intervals to ensure you apply when you are meant to.

31

HOW ARE EXPENSES SHARED?

Money is the most common cause of conflict in relationships of all kinds, and co-writing relationships are no exception. People have very different comfort levels when they talk about money and also different priorities when it comes to spending it.

It's important to be clear and up-front about what expenses are associated with your shared projects, how much they will be, and who will be responsible for paying them. We can never predict every situation, so it's important to put a process in place for reviewing proposed expenses and making decisions with your partner.

The questions that can arise are varied, virtually unlimited and possibly unexpected.

For instance, if your team agrees to use Word for editing but one author has an older version of the software that isn't compatible with the current one, will that author be responsible for the cost to upgrade, or will it be a shared business expense?

If you're writing non-fiction, what about the costs of research materials or travel for interviews?

Can you categorize the expenses that will be the responsibility of both partners and those that will fall to one co-author?

What if Author A has solid cash flow but little time, while Author B has more time than money to invest in the co-author relationship? Their agreement may put Author B in charge of the marketing-related tasks, while Author A will contribute a cash equivalent to the extra hours put in by their partner, to purchase ads and marketing software (such as subscriptions to Canva and BookBrush).

Remember what we said earlier—fair doesn't always mean the same. As long as both co-authors are comfortable with the arrangement and agree in advance that this approach will work, that's fair.

Here are a few key tips for keeping the management of expenses out of the conflict zone.

Discuss your money style

Just as it's important to discuss your conflict resolution style, it can be useful to self-reflect and then discuss how you and your co-author feel about money. Books such as *You Are a Badass At Making Money* by Jen Sincero can give you a place to start that discussion, with questions that help you figure out your comfort and risk tolerance with money.

Never make assumptions

Don't assume your writing partner's financial situation or attitudes about money are the same as yours. Nothing breaks a partnership faster than money conflict. Imagine your partner committing to that rock-star cover designer you both covet without first asking if you're willing and able to pay 50% of the US$800 invoice.

Always agree in advance

Never spend money on the project without agreeing in advance. While you might think investing US$1000 in a BookBub Feature Deal is a great gamble, your co-author may have another idea—or a lower risk tolerance. And, while they may believe they've found the app to end all apps for scheduling social media, you may know of a better deal or even have a subscription you can use for your joint project. You just never know. If you do see a once-in-a-lifetime super sale on something you have to act on right now, consider the following before talking to your co-author:

1. Is the purchase returnable if I assumed wrong and my co-author's not willing to pay their portion?
2. Am I willing to pay for all of it myself if my co-author's not in agreement?

Track your time and inputs

To determine if your co-authored projects are helping you meet your author goals (and assuming you're not doing it 100% for fun), it's a good idea to track not only your financial but also your time contributions to the project.

Imagine spending 100 hours on a book project that makes $300 in royalties in the first year while your portion of the indie publishing and marketing expenses cost $1000.

Not every project is done for the purposes of generating revenue, so that may be fine with you. But you can't make an informed cost-benefit decision if (a) you don't have the data; and (b) you haven't set clear outcome and performance goals.

And it is valuable to track the actuals of your time and money investment in your project for more than your own value analysis. Research tells us that our human brains tend to overestimate our contributions to joint projects and underestimate everyone else's contribution. *Ahem.* Tracking the actual time (and how many words) you're contributing to your co-authored project will make for easier discussions about workload and task distribution within your partnership.

Assign a dollar value to time

One of the things that has worked well within our Creative Academy writing partnership has been assigning a dollar value to certain tasks.

Hypothetically, let's say it would cost us $35 to 50 an hour to hire someone to do our bookkeeping and accounting. If one of our co-author partners had the skills and desire to take on that job, they could log the time and bill the partnership for their work instead of hiring it out.

In fact, that's exactly what happened! Crystal researched what it would cost to hire a pro to do the work she'd been doing for our partnership for three years without compensation. She approached the team and suggested we could either outsource the job or pay her. It was a no-brainer (well, a three-brainer), and now she is being fairly compensated for her extra admin time.

We also have a guideline that if two of us would like to do the same job, we either figure out a way to split the task or find two equivalent jobs and discuss which makes more sense for which party. We base that decision on preference, skill set and availability.

Agree on a working currency

Plenty of co-author partnerships are cross-border ventures with partners from different countries. As we mentioned in the previous sections, if you're sharing expenses, you need to agree on your primary working currency.

Managing exchange rates can be tricky. Some accountants want to know the exact amount of an expense at the time of exchange. Others will allow clients to use the annual average exchange rate for a tax-filing year. Know what your accountant or bookkeeper expects so, at tax filing time, you're not looking up exchange rates for dozens of dates in the previous fiscal year.

Agree on boundaries and limits

If you and your partners have decided to run ads on your books, be sure to agree on an upper limit to what you're willing and able to spend each month, and review this amount regularly.

Each month, our co-author team meets to discuss our publishing business. We review our ad spends across platforms and make strategy decisions for the upcoming month.

With respect to billing for bookkeeping time, we know from Crystal's experience that it can vary from month to month (with more time required at year end), but averages about three hours per month. We could have asked her to bill for her actual time, but we feel comfortable with a three-hour average per month, so that's how we manage that recurring expense.

Our team has a great deal of experience with publishing tasks. We used our knowledge to calculate the average time it takes to prep a book for publication and set that figure as our upper limit of what one of our co-authors can submit to our publishing business to cover the costs to complete that task.

The takeaway here is that there is no absolutely right or wrong way to set boundaries. Find methods that work for everyone in your partnership, review them as needed, and celebrate not doing work that does not bring you joy!

Play the what-if game

Yes—again with the what-if game. In case you can't tell, we love this game.

Anytime you're discussing expenditure guidelines in your partnership, it's a good idea to play the what-if game. Here's a real example from our Creative Academy Guides for Writers series.

We agreed to spend up to $1000 per month on Amazon ads, out of our shared bank account, for those titles that pay us equal royalties. But, with three or more books to advertise and four primary countries (Canada, the USA, the UK, Australia) in which to spend ad dollars, $1000 can be split in many ways.

What if the ads on one book are working well? Should we spend more than that book's "fair share" of the ad budget?

What if our ad spend on a title isn't giving us a good return on investment (ROI)?

- Should we reduce the spend?
- If so, by how much?
- Should we change the targets?
- If so, how much time should we invest in finding new targets and creating new ads?

What if our ads are doing really well and we spend our monthly budget before month end?

- Should we increase the budget temporarily?
- Should we increase it permanently?
- Should we leave it as is?

What if one of the co-authors wants to run ads on a book that is not within our shared co-author royalty agreement?

- How will we distinguish those ads on the expenses payable?
- How will we track our ad manager's time?

For each what-if scenario you think of, you need to agree on a solution that all partners are comfortable with.

Keep your receipts

You have to save receipts to keep your accountant and the government happy when you claim those writing and publishing expenses as a tax write-off. But that proof of money spent on your partnership keeps you accountable to your co-authors as well.

And, if you decide to dissolve the co-author partnership, your receipts will indicate which assets were purchased by individuals for the benefit of the partnership, and which were purchased jointly. It makes cancelling or divvying up assets a lot cleaner.

When we say "save receipts," we're suggesting a system that's more professional and organized than tossing slips of paper into a shoebox—although shoebox filing is better than no system at all.

Keep your records transparent

All partners should have easy access to your partnership's accounting of expenses, including what each partner has been paid and their portion of shared business expenses.

You don't need a formal accounting program to do this—a shared Google Sheet will do the trick. Make sure it tracks project-related expenditures, the date they were paid, who paid them, whether or not they were shared expenses, and the currency used. Do not include the access information (passwords) for shared accounts in this document for security reasons.

Review shared credit cards and accounts regularly

It's important to review shared credit cards and bank accounts each month. When co-authors share financial accounts, it can happen that a charge is accidentally put on the wrong card, or that you are charged for something in error but assume it was something your co-author bought. And then there's data theft, which happens more often than we'd like to think about.

Make sure you're being a responsible business partner by keeping all passwords, financial information and cards in a safe place and checking in on them regularly to make sure all is as it should be.

Your Turn

Look back through this chapter at the questions we've provided.

- What is your process for spending money that impacts your co-authors?
- How often will you review your shared finance and accounts?
- Do all partners have access to your financial accounts and expense summaries?
- What is the process for tracking and storing receipts and expenses?
- Are there any billable tasks within your publishing partnership that a partner can assume responsibility for?
- If yes, at what rate should they be billed?
- What is the upper limit of time or dollars that can be billed?
- What is the working currency for financial calculations in your partnership?

- Play the what-if game with your co-authors around other issues to do with publishing expenses.
- Brainstorm solutions that will work for everyone on your team.

32

HOW WILL YOU MANAGE SHARED ASSETS?

During the course of your writing and publishing activities, you will likely generate assets that are shared and make purchases that belong to the partnership. You need to have a plan in place to manage those assets.

Digital assets

Producing and publishing books creates a lot of digital assets. The ones you own—your book's files—should be carefully backed up and stored so that everyone who needs them can have access. We talked about backing up your work already.

For digital assets you share—like tools or software that you use in your business—make sure each partner has the access they need. Your working agreements should explain what will happen with digital assets if and when you dissolve the partnership.

Storing digital files can be expensive, and if your books are heavy on the graphics, you'll need to know who will be responsible for paying for the storage necessary to keep those safely backed up.

Physical assets

If your partnership purchases equipment or keeps physical books on hand, it's important to know where that stock will be stored and who is responsible for it. A shared spreadsheet that records the partnership assets each person has is a valuable tool.

Your Turn

- Are you keeping physical book stock on hand? Who owns that physical stock?
- Who is responsible for replacing stock that is stolen or destroyed in a fire or flood?
- Is the stock insured? Who is responsible for paying for and maintaining that insurance?

33

HOW DO AGENTS AND EDITORS VIEW CO-WRITTEN BOOKS?

You may be wondering—do agents or editors care if a book is co-written? Does it make any difference to them? The answer, like many things in publishing, comes down to a very vague "it depends."

There are agents and editors in publishing houses who have had great experiences with co-written projects, and others who have been burned by the process. It can be useful to understand the pros and cons from the agent's and editor's perspectives.

Advantages

Two brains are better than one

All the reasons an author might enjoy working with a co-writer also impact the publishing team in a positive way. The two (or more) authors can double up on creativity and keep each other balanced and on track during the creative process.

Promotion plus

Two authors create an opportunity to double up on promotion by reaching out to their communities and dividing the work needed to promote a book.

An established brand

If one of the authors is established, or if the book is part of a shared world, the publishing house may have an easier time—not easy, mind you; nothing is easy in publishing—selling the book to retailers or readers and recouping their costs.

Challenges

Communication

Two authors might require double the amount of communication to ensure no one is left off email strings and everyone is included in decision-making processes.

Determining responsibility

With two authors involved in a project, there needs to be clarity about who is responsible for different aspects of the publishing process. Will both writers respond to requests and questions from the agent or editor, or will there be a single contact?

Deadlines

Publishing involves a series of deadlines that extend beyond the submission of the manuscript. There will be a deadline for revisions, a deadline for approval of the cover and back-of-book copy, a deadline for acceptance of galley proofs, and so on. These timelines are not typically extended just because two authors are involved. This means that the agent or editor must rely on the authors to work together efficiently to meet those deadlines.

Payments

Ensuring that royalties and payments are split between two authors adds a layer of complexity and paperwork.

Agent co-ordination

Does each co-author have their own agent? If so, which agent will take this project out to publishers? One agent may need to communicate with the other agent to ensure everything is covered. In most cases, an agent will require both co-authors to have a written collaboration agreement that outlines the division of tasks, financial splits, and procedures if one author no longer wants to continue with the project.

The most important takeaway for any co-writing team is that the more prepared you are to take advantage of the positives, and the more steps you've taken to handle problems before they arise, the more likely it is that your agent or editor will see your co-writing relationship as a good thing.

Your Turn

- Have you and your co-writer addressed the issues raised in the previous sections so you can present a professional working agreement to your editor or agent if they ask?
- Do you or your co-writer have an agent relationship? If so, have those agents been informed about this project?
- If you're seeking representation for your co-authored project, you can find tips on how to secure an agent in *Full Time Author*.

34

HOW DO YOU QUERY A CO-WRITTEN BOOK?

If you are considering traditional publishing for your co-written book, you'll need to write a query letter. This letter will be used to either attract an agent or editor, or clarify your project to an agent or editor you have already worked with. Yes, the dreaded query letter is helpful even if you already have an agent. It provides you with an opportunity to sell the project so they understand how they can promote it to publishers. If you have an agent, your query will likely be far more casual, but it's still a valuable tool.

The book *Full Time Author* describes in greater detail what an agent does, and explains why you may want to work with one. There is no "right choice," because what ultimately matters are your aspirations for your writing career—and this goes back to your outcome goal.

Both Donna and Crystal have managed their careers independently. Eileen has chosen to work with an agent. All three of us have had success. However, if you want to traditionally publish with one of the larger houses (Penguin,

RandomHouse, HarperCollins), you typically require an agent to get your work in front of an editor for consideration.

The goal of your query

Based on what we've gleaned running a community of over 1,000 authors for the last three years, the only thing writers hate more than writing a story synopsis (and kale) is writing query letters. (Okay, it was Eileen who added kale to the hate list).

The challenge with a query letter is to distill several hundred pages of a book—written in blood, sweat and tears—into one page. It's enough to make an author cry.

It's most helpful to remember that the overall goal of a query letter is *not* to share *everything* about your book. The goal is to intrigue the agent or editor and entice them to read more. You need to ensure you've communicated the genre, word count, main character and stakes of the story. (Non-fiction is a bit different, but we'll discuss that below.)

However, what one agent likes in a query letter can drive another agent crazy. Some love comparable titles like "this book is Jane Austen meets Indiana Jones." (We'd love to read the adventuring Lizzie Bennet in great dresses.) Others hate them. Some agents want to know why you chose to query them, and others don't care.

What's an author to do? To start, read the agent's website, where they detail what they are looking for in a query and how to submit. Secondly, when in doubt, go with a query that you feel best represents your work without trying to get too clever or creative: no glitter, no GIFs. And yes, we know agents who have seen both.

Eileen's agent, Barbara Poelle, has a simple formula that may help. She wants to see three things in a query: the hook, the book and the cook.

The hook—This is the one-line catchphrase that sums up your book. For those of you old enough to remember *TV Guide*, the hook would be the short description to go with each show. *Jaws*, for example, would be "A giant killer shark terrorizes a seaside community." *The Wizard of Oz* would be "A young girl is whisked away to a magical land where she must figure out how to get back home." If an agent likes comparable titles, this is often where you could place that element in your query.

The book—Talk about your main character, what they want and what gets in their way. Tell us what the stakes are if your character is unsuccessful. This part of the query is typically the longest, but it is still unlikely to be more than two or three paragraphs.

The cook—End your query with a bit of information about yourself and your co-author. This is a chance to share any skills or abilities that make you the perfect authors to write this book —it's where you can let your personalities shine through.

A perfect example of this comes from a Creative Academy member, Bonnie Jacoby, who sums up her YA fantasy query with, "I totally believe dragons are real and they will return. I intend to be their champion against extinction." It hints at the humour in her book and feels fresh and fun. Heck, it makes her sound like fun to work with, and that is never a bad thing.

There are many resources that help you write a query letter. While there are some books on the topic, you'll typically find more current examples on blogs and on websites. The Query Shark blog by literary agent Janet Reid has a wealth of resources and is a great place to start.

One of the best things that you can do with your query is get other eyes on it. People who have read the book can comment on if it captures what you've written, and people who have no idea what the book is about can tell you what they took away from the query alone.

At The Creative Academy for Writers, we often critique each other's queries to help capture the story and make sure no typos escape notice before we send them out. If you're not a member (gosh, why not?), share your query with your writing group or another source for feedback.

Non-fiction book proposals

If you're pitching a non-fiction book, you'll need a query letter *and* a book proposal. There are entire books on this subject. *Non-Fiction Book Proposals Anybody Can Write* (revised), by Elizabeth Lyon, is one you might consider. You can also try online resources, including blogs by agents and writing organizations.

At its most basic level, a non-fiction proposal is a business plan for your book. It typically includes the following elements.

Target audience or market

The answer here is never *everyone*. That's too vague and also not true. While we all hope everyone likes our books, who is the actual target? Who is the book most likely to appeal to?

Comparative title analysis

What other books are already published that may be similar? This isn't about trashing other titles. You would never say something like "*Title* XYZ is similar except it's poorly written trash and my book is genius." Instead you need to show that there are other books on this topic and explain how yours compares.

You may think that saying "There is nothing out there like this!" would be a good thing, but it's not. It leaves the agent or editor wondering if there is any need or desire for this kind of book. They may also assume you haven't done the required research in your field.

Marketing plan

What are the specific things that you plan to do to promote your co-authored book? Do you or your co-author have an existing platform (audience) that you can reach out to? For example, if you are writing a book on writing, what writing organizations do you belong to? Where are the places that writers hang out? Do you speak at writing conferences, or teach? You would include all of these connections in your marketing plan.

Bio

Why are you the best team to write this book? What in your joint backgrounds gives you the qualifications or expertise to give advice on this subject? This is especially important if you're writing a self-help book such as *How to Regain Your Health and Well-Being*. Is one of you a nutritionist? A doctor? A well-established fitness trainer?

Overview of the book

The overview provides the big picture of the themes you intend to cover in your book.

Outline

Your outline is simply a list of the chapters and topics to cover.

Sample chapters

Typically, agents and editors want to see one to three chapters of a manuscript to gauge your writing style and voice.

Whew! That feels like a lot, doesn't it? Here's the good news—if you're writing non-fiction, you typically don't need to write the entire book in order to sell it. Many non-fiction books are purchased on proposal alone. The downside is that if you sign a contract and take money, the publisher will expect you to deliver that book on time—so if deadlines give you hives and send your muse running, you may want to write the whole thing before you pitch.

If you're writing fiction, you can take a deep breath. You don't need to do a proposal. However, it never hurts to think about how you would promote the book and what comparable titles are out there. It's also unlikely that you will sell a novel on proposal. Even with an outline, it's much more difficult to see how a story will play out. Unless you have an established relationship with a publisher, you're unlikely to gain much traction pitching a novel based solely on a proposal.

Queries for a co-written book

If you've written queries before, the good news is that a query for a co-written book isn't that different. If you look at Barbara's Poelle's suggested format of hook, book and cook, the only real difference is in the section on the cook.

Instead of discussing one author, you'll indicate that the book is co-written and provide a bio on each of the authors. At the end of the query, you'll "sign" from both authors, although one co-author may be the designated contact for initial correspondence.

You may consider creating a shared email account, PenName@gmail.com, for example, that you can both access.

How will you divide this job?

Like you do with every task in your write-edit-publish-promote business, figure out how you and your co-author will divvy up the job of submitting your work and pursuing publication.

Who will write your query and synopsis? Who will research agents? How will you keep track of who you have submitted to, and when? Will you get a post office box for written replies or a shared email address for digital submissions?

Your Turn

- Do you and your co-author want an agent? Why or why not?
- How would you describe the hook, the book and the cooks of your manuscript? How would your co-writer?
- If you or your co-author already has an agent, book a time to talk with them about your co-written project and discuss whether it's something they would want to represent.
- If you are writing non-fiction, discuss with your co-author the elements of a proposal and determine who will take on writing each section.
- Who in your partnership will be responsible for tracking submissions and responses?

35

HOW WILL YOU KEEP THINGS RUNNING SMOOTHLY?

Once you've set up your business and writing partnership, it's important to know how best to maintain the momentum you've created.

Regular progress reviews

Checking in on a regular basis with your publishing business, like glancing down at a map as you travel, ensures you're still on track to reach your outcome goal. How often you need to perform progress reviews depends on your working process and the level of co-operative working you do.

In our case, we meet once a month to review progress on writing and publishing for the various books in our Creative Academy Guides for Writers series, to get our marketing homework for the next 30 days and to review and make decisions about new promotional opportunities.

In addition, every three months (once per quarter), we meet for a full day to do long-range planning and decide on focus projects, in both our personal writing careers and our shared writing business, for the next 12 weeks. Doing this together helps us all stay up to date with each other's lives and lets us flex our goals to work well for all of our partners.

There's no right way to do this, though—you should meet only as often as you need and want to. For us, writing together and getting together is part of the fun of working as a team, and we find that many of our best ideas come out of those in-person check-ins.

Below, we discuss some benefits of regular check-ins.

Opportunity to head off conflict

Conflict is tricky. It grows in the dark if you ignore it. Something small that used to be mildly irritating can become this creature that's out of control. By touching base on a regular basis, you can talk through any potential conflicts and resolve them.

Progress check-in

Hey, we get it. Life happens. You plan to spend the next week with your head down getting the pages in and then your dog gets into a rumble with a raccoon *again*, despite the fact you've told them to leave the trash pandas alone, and you spend that week at the vet hospital, awaiting surgery results, and then chasing down your dog to ensure they don't chew the stitches out. (Good thing dogs are cute because they are not the brightest.) A progress check-in allows you to share the actual progress made versus the intended progress.

Story discussions

Setting aside time to talk through story issues is helpful. You can outline a book in extensive detail, but we all know what happens once you start writing. Our imaginary friends have this habit of running off and doing what they want—things that may not be in the carefully planned outline. Having a regular check-in allows you and your co-author to explore any potential story directions you didn't see at the start and decide if you'd like to make changes to the outline.

Publication discussions

Are there decisions related to your book publication that you need to make? Are there upcoming deadlines for uploading your manuscript? Do you need to review the effectiveness of your ads? Touching base on your publication process allows you to make timely decisions.

Identification of priorities

At The Creative Academy for Writers, we encourage members to check in and make plans in 12-week blocks. This isn't just because we like to see them at the retreat (although we always love to hear what they're up to) but because it's easier to identify priorities in shorter-term blocks.

You typically can see 12 weeks ahead without requiring a crystal ball. Are there holidays coming up? Other demands on your time? While we all want to do *all the things*, we have to focus. What will have your attention in the coming weeks? What are the most important upcoming tasks? This doesn't just include writing priorities, but also those related to the publication and marketing of your book.

Division of tasks

Who will do what tasks in the coming weeks? Having a clear delineation of responsibility ensures that you don't double up on work or drop a ball because you think the other person is taking it on.

At The Creative Academy for Writers, our admin team meets regularly to review the progress of all our publishing and business projects. It's our chance to celebrate, plot out next steps and see how everyone is faring.

In an ideal world, these progress check-ins would take place face to face, but distance (and the occasional global pandemic) may make this impossible for your co-authoring relationship. While the purpose of our meetings is to cover the business topics, it's also a chance to connect on a personal level, which is invaluable in maintaining our fabulous working relationships.

Celebration of wins

It may seem like we're always looking for a chance to bust out the champagne—and who are we kidding, bubbles make everything more exciting—but celebration is important. The publishing road is a bumpy one. Taking time to celebrate your wins helps lift everyone's spirits for the challenges ahead. Further, it creates a bond between team members, a sense that we're in this together. And did we mention bubbles make everything more fun? So if you can meet in person, consider ending the meeting with a dinner out, a bowling night or a spa visit. We can always recommend champagne.

Your Turn

Ensure that you review not only your co-author relationship and project, but also how co-authoring fits into your personal writing goals and time.

- How often will you meet with your writing partners to review your project progress? We recommend every 12 weeks at a minimum.
- Are you still happy with the amount of time that the co-authored project takes from your available work time?
- What do you anticipate your workload will look like in the coming weeks?

- You can download the Sample Progress Review Template Google Doc online at CreativeAcademyForWriters.com/resources and complete it on your own.
- Once you and your co-authors have completed the progress review, discuss your answers and adjust your process and expectations as necessary to keep everything running smoothly.

36

HOW WILL YOU HANDLE CONFLICT?

Remember your first real, true love? The time you fell head over heels with someone and you knew in your soul that the universe had brought the two of you together in some kind of divine, meant-to-be, once-in-a-lifetime true love that would last forever?

Yeah.

Then, perhaps, you noticed they had this habit of chewing really, really loudly. Or you went away to summer camp and met your new, *new* true love. Perhaps they crushed your wee heart for the first time and you thought you'd never love again.

This is a reminder that when you are in the heady new days of a co-authoring relationship, you may not imagine that things could ever be problematic. You can't fathom that their chewing sounds would ever not be completely adorable. But they will be. Oh, yes… they will, and you'll feel like you've partnered with a cow chewing cud. Most people don't expect relationships to fall apart until they do.

If you didn't read the section How Do You Resolve Conflicts in The Writing Process?, or the section What Contracts Do You

Need in Place Before You Get Started?, go back and read them now. (Go on. We'll wait here.) We can't underscore enough the importance of planning for conflict before it happens and having clear contracts. So many of the challenges that can break up a co-working relationship can be avoided with a clear outline of expectations and guidelines on how to address challenges.

Here are some challenges that might lead to the breakup of a co-author relationship.

- Wanting different things in the writing or business relationship
- Creative conflict
- Personality conflict
- Publication process or direction conflict
- Feeling unfairly treated in a multi-person partnership
- Feeling that the benefits of the relationship don't outweigh the challenges
- Failure of one co-author to complete tasks by a deadline or to a certain level of quality
- Divergence of direction

You can add endless additional conflicts here. People can fight and disagree about the most random things.

Importance of conflict negotiation

Business relationships, like any relationship, will have conflict. And remember, conflict can be a good thing for all of us—not just for our characters when they need a little torturing. We know that our imaginary friends need conflict in order to grow, and we're no different. As your co-authoring relationship moves forward, there will naturally be friction points.

We wrote this book in part because we believe that many aspects of conflict between co-authors can be predicted. Talking through the areas that might be challenging, and establishing guidelines to handle those situations, can nip conflicts in the bud, or in some cases prevent them altogether.

Agreeing on how to handle conflict when it does arise is also important. The ability to talk through the issue calmly using a win-win approach will help you keep small conflicts from growing into deal breakers.

Basic conflict-resolution tips

There are many great resources on conflict resolution. One of the classics is the book *Getting to Yes* by Roger Fisher and William Ury. But below we've included a few quick and easy tips.

Respond in a timely fashion

Conflicts can fester. Like leftovers pushed to the back of the fridge, nothing good is going to happen if you ignore them. You need to drag these issues out and deal with them.

Consider time and place

Yes, we just told you not to not allow things to fester, but consider the time and place that you choose to have a difficult discussion. Try to ensure that you have enough time to fully address the issue and that it's in a place where both people feel safe and comfortable.

Use I not you language

A classic piece of advice when discussing a conflict is to speak in the first person. When you are discussing what bothers you, use *I* language: "I feel X when Y happens."

This is better than *you* language: "When you do X, I want to scream."

You language can put people on the defensive because they feel blamed. When you use *I* language, others are more likely to listen.

Avoid always *and* never

"You always do X." "I never get to do Y."

The problem with *always* and *never* statements is that the other person will immediately remember the one time that they *didn't* do that thing they supposedly *always* do—or *did* do the thing they've been accused of *never* doing.

The actual issue isn't that something happens *every* time, but that it happens often enough to create tension in the relationship.

Avoid inflammatory language

Arguments escalate. They tend to start out small and then, as one person raises their voice, the other person often raises their voice to meet or exceed the other person's volume. Once you use any kind of name calling or volume to make your point, the other person is that much more likely to respond with the same —and before you know it, things are spinning out of control.

Plan for a win-win

Conflict resolution is often about negotiation. Your goal shouldn't be to "win" but rather to find a solution that allows everyone to feel the response is satisfactory.

Walking away while keeping it classy

Ending a co-author relationship doesn't have to be a negative thing. Relationships, even good ones, can have a life span. It's possible you and your co-author had a great thing going, but now one or both of you have adjusted your outcome goal. Or perhaps one of you has gotten a new job and no longer has time to invest in the co-author project.

We've all been through relationship breakups, and we understand the desire to burn it to the ground if it's ending in a way you didn't want or choose. Your emotion-flooded brain might be whispering in your ear to leave a one-star review for the other person's books, or slam them in your writers group after after one too many glasses of wine. But this drama is only entertaining for others. It never reflects well on you.

Publishing is a business in a relatively small ecosystem. You never know how people are connected or who might know someone else. Take the advice about dealing with conflict that Eileen's mom gave her—"Keep it classy so you can always hold your head high." Trust that karma will take care of everything else.

If it is your co-author who handles the breakup badly, don't give in to a desire to retaliate. Instead, keep careful notes of interactions. Ensure agreements are in writing to reduce the chance of miscommunication.

Your Turn

- Journal about conflicts you've had with people in the past.
- What is your typical conflict response?
- How have past conflicts been resolved?
- What would you do differently?
- Discuss possible areas of conflict with your co-writer. Do either of you have issues that trigger you? Identifying these will make you more aware when they come up, and better able to address them quickly.
- Do you and your co-writer have a conflict-resolution plan outlined in your contract?
- Consider scheduling regular progress reviews throughout the project to check in and ensure conflicts are resolved before they grow into three-headed monsters.

37
HOW AND WHEN WILL YOU END THE PARTNERSHIP?

We've discussed the importance of knowing your why and being clear about your outcome, process and performance goals when setting out on a publishing project. A portion of that planning involves deciding how long you'll continue a co-authoring relationship and when it will come to an end. To continue the dating and marriage analogy we've had going for a while, this section is about considering your pre-nup. You may head into that co-author marriage with every intention to be together forever, or you could intend for this to be a short-term connection.

Ending things after one project

There are a number of reasons that you may do only a single project with a co-writer. It's possible that the project is a one-off, a book that doesn't lend itself to a series or further books. It's also possible that you have picked up an opportunity to write a shared book that fits perfectly between your own writing goals or fills an economic need.

The upside of a one-book agreement is that it's time limited. Even if a relationship is less than ideal, or the experience not what you hoped, it's often possible to focus and finish. If you're unsure if you would like co-authoring, a time-limited or project-limited experience is a great place to start.

The downside is that you will have invested a lot of time and effort into a co-authoring agreement, and you may feel frustrated if this lasts for only one project. Furthermore, producing only one book together will not allow you to build a readership over time as a team.

Ending things after a set time period or number of books

Another option for co-authors is to go into the agreement with a set number of projects in mind. That is, you may agree that there will be three books in a series or that you want to co-author a limited number of travel guides to specific destinations. You might also state in your agreement that, after the agreed-upon number of projects are completed, you may extend it depending on interest and success.

Or your agreement may place a time limitation on your partnership, stating that you've set up X period to complete this project. For example, "We will co-author as many travel guides as can be completed in the next five years."

One upside of this approach is that it allows you to create a plan for how this set number of books can be used to promote each co-author. It also allows you, over time, to perfect the systems you create to co-write and co-publish. You'll likely find that, with each new book, your efficiency increases, as does the ease with which you work together.

When we decided to write The Creative Academy Guides for Writers, we initially agreed to a three-book commitment, with an option to write more titles in the series if it made business sense and we enjoyed the process. Since this is our sixth book—and we have at least six more in different stages of writing and development—it's clear our co-author relationship is going well.

Now, instead of talking about whether we'll write more together, we plan in terms of time—what do we agree to write and publish in the next year? As we've mentioned, we meet quarterly to update goals and assess personal and shared obligations that impact our publishing business.

One downside of this model is that you may find yourself locked into an agreement to produce a set number of books even if your interests or priorities have shifted. Conversely, your writing partner may wish to focus on a different part of their author career and may not feel as committed as you are to the joint project.

Ending things after meeting a budget or revenue target

It may be that your partnership has a revenue-based goal, and you've agreed that once a certain income target is met, you won't invest any more marketing funds or time writing future books.

You may be pragmatic and decide to use market interest as the indicator that propels or ends your co-author relationship. If readers aren't engaged with your books, if you don't have read-through in a series, that might be a rationale to end the relationship—or, if you enjoy working together, to pivot and write in a new genre.

Keeping the end of the partnership open-ended

The final option is that you and your co-writer set an agreement that is open—you each express an interest in working together until that interest is no longer shared.

The upside of this arrangement is that it's the most flexible. It allows you to continue if you're having success and not feel locked down if the project seems to be waning.

The downside of an open-ended arrangement is that there is no firm plan beyond the current project. For individuals who like to have a clear sense of their work priorities a year or two into the future, this can be frustrating. They may feel reluctant to invest in tools, resources or even a working relationship without a sense of how long it might last.

Many people have a hard time clearly communicating their wants and needs once they're deep into a partnership. Negotiating terms before you have an emotional and practical investment in the shared project helps avoid disappointment.

And, by building in regular meetings for review and reflection, everyone can stay up to date on how people are feeling, air issues in a positive environment, and keep the partnership beneficial to all.

Dissolving a relationship that isn't working

Any number of reasons can trigger one or both partners in a co-author relationship to look at each other and think, "You know, I don't want to do this anymore."

This may happen during the writing process or following publication. Regardless, all parties need to determine how to wind things down.

If nothing has been published and you're on good terms, you can make the decision then go for drinks to mourn your loss (or celebrate your freedom). Think of this like walking away from a relationship before you've bought any worldly goods together.

If you have co-published a book, things may be more complicated—but they don't have to be difficult.

Will you take the book out of print if it is indie published?

If not, how will you continue to track sales and revenue? Like negotiating custody of a child, you'll need to decide who has what responsibilities for your "book baby" after you split up.

Case Study: Donna Barker and Tony Ollivier

Here's an example of how and why a fabulous co-author partnership might end before the book is published.

When Donna and Tony were working on the second draft of their book, they had differing opinions about a core aspect of the heroine's personality. This had been a low-simmering issue for a few months, and both were happy to compromise a little, being very Canadian and polite.

But when it came time to share the story with beta readers, Donna was no longer happy to see a scene that created discomfort for some readers acted out on the page. Tony stood his ground and reminded Donna about the kind of book she'd agreed to co-author.

Tony was right; the character's actions were in keeping with the genre.

But Donna was also right in wanting the changes since, over their months of writing together and researching the market, they realized that the genre they'd been writing could not be advertised on Amazon or Facebook.

It was a moment of recognizing a hard truth—that they had written a reasonably good story that was not going to serve their shared outcome goal, which was to make money from their co-authored book. Ouch. They figured out which scenes needed to be dialed back and started a significant rewrite.

Their co-author relationship continued to be positive and fun. And then life threw a wrench in the works. Tony's work situation changed, and he had much less time to invest in their book. In the same month, his publisher sent back revision notes for his contracted title. The duo agreed to set their project aside for six months.

In that time, Donna found other projects to fill her time and wrote a romance novel on her own. She also had a plan to write and release two more full-length novels in the six months that followed.

When Donna and Tony sat down again to discuss their co-authored project, they realized their title would not serve either of their author careers as a stand-alone since it wasn't in a genre that their audiences read—Tony's being suspense, Donna's being contemporary romance.

It was a hard decision to formally end the co-author partnership because they really did enjoy working together. But since neither was writing just for fun, it no longer made sense, from an author-career point of view, to continue. (Insert tears here.)

When one co-author wants to leave the partnership and the other doesn't

One of the most challenging situations can be if one co-author wants to end the partnership, but the other doesn't. Resolving this situation will depend on how much you've co-written and published, and how formalized your working agreement and business structure are.

If you registered your partnership as a legal business, your partnership agreement should include instructions on how to deal with this contingency. There is likely a clause detailing the process for one partner buying out another.

How you registered your copyrights will also impact how you need to handle intellectual property. If your books have copyrights registered by the business, that is much different than if each person has copyrighted their own works.

No doubt, discussions will need to be had, hopefully without lawyers. We can't imagine all the situations that could arise, but since we're experts at the what-if game, we came up with a few scenarios to give you a sense of what you might need to consider.

- *What if* Writer A wants to keep writing those travel guides long after Writer B is done with the project? Can the guides maintain the same branding?
- *What if* Writer A wants to work with a new co-author who has a different approach to writing the guides?
- *What if* you created a fictional world with a co-author and they want to continue writing in that world with a different co-author?
- *What if* that new co-author wants to bring in new world or story elements that you feel would negatively impact your current author brand? (Your name will still be connected to the series.)

The more you discuss these issues before there is a conflict situation, the more likely you are to navigate the end of the relationship smoothly.

Dissolving the relationship when someone dies

Yeah, we know. The last thing you want to think about is the demise of your writing partner, or the thought that something unexpected could happen to you.

But copyright lasts a very long time. Like, almost an entire lifetime past the death of the author. Things could get complicated if you haven't planned for this outcome or addressed it in your contracts and your will.

The question is: what will happen to your intellectual property when you're no longer able to look after it?

Unless you've specified otherwise, your copyright in a work will be passed along to whoever inherits your estate. But what does that mean for the books you've co-authored? Who will have decision-making power about those titles? Will you be sharing it with someone who has no idea what it means to manage publications? It's a scary thought.

Here are a few questions to ponder. Make sure your answers are worked into one of your written agreements.

- Can the surviving author finish works-in-progress that had been under discussion or partly finished at the time of death? How will you manage copyright and royalty distribution if that does happen?
- Can the surviving author(s) keep writing in the world or series?
- How much involvement (if any) will the inheritor of the deceased author's share of copyright and royalties have in ongoing business decisions?
- Who has control of and access to the publishing accounts, if they are shared?
- What happens if the author who was handling publishing, royalty payouts, and administration is the one who dies?
- Will copyright ownership be transferred to the surviving co-author for existing published works?

Your Turn

- What is your ideal scenario for wrapping up a co-author relationship?
- How does your writing partner feel?
- What safeguards might you put in place if the situation changes?
- Have you considered the unconsiderable?
- Have you spoken about your options with a lawyer who has copyright expertise?

38

HOW WILL YOU DEAL WITH SUCCESS?

In this book, we've asked you to plan for everything from minor conflict to a bus that takes out your business partner. But it's time to switch things up and end on a high note. We often make plans for what will happen if something doesn't work, but what about planning for success and growth?

Take a moment and visualize your project wildly exceeding your expectations.

- Sales explode out of the gate.
- Your book reviews are all five-star, and word of mouth is viral.
- You hit a bestseller list.
- Readers are clamouring for more and more books.
- Foreign publishers want to license the book.
- There's a bidding war to make your book into a miniseries.
- Ryan Reynolds calls and begs to be the star of your story. (Did you doubt that Eileen would find some way to sneak her Ryan Reynolds fantasy into this book? If so, then you failed to realize the depth of her love.)

- Your series is winning awards.
- Money is bunching up in your accounts; you open your wallet and hundred-dollar bills fall out.
- Conferences beg you to come and share your wisdom.
- When you give readings, there are lines around the block, including people dressed up like your characters. Some of these readers cry when they meet you because they're so excited.

That feels good, doesn't it? Pause a moment and enjoy it. Eileen is taking a moment to picture a nice dinner with Ryan as they discuss the miniseries project and how he's smitten with her. (Then Donna shows up and ruins the moment since she, too, has a shameless crush on Ryan Reynolds.)

But wait.

All that success comes with different challenges. There's increased pressure to write more books. To hit that list again. You attract a lot of attention, which also (sadly) means you attract envious people who want to chip away at your success. Managing your business requires more time and possibly more help. More help means having to manage assistants or employees.

Not to mention Ryan's suddenly wanting to go to dinner all the time. But he only wants to go with Eileen, and Donna is wicked jealous. Hey, it's not Eileen's fault she's so delightful.

Success is great, and it is what we all hope for, but it's important to plan for some of the complications that come with it.

When planning future projects in The Creative Academy for Writers and with our book series, Crystal often challenges Donna and Eileen to think not only about how all our systems could break due to failed ventures, but also how they could break if we're successful.

How easy will it be to scale up our systems? Will the membership tracking system that we chose when we had less than 50 members manage the thousands of people who join after reading our books? What should we plan for if all goes well? How will we pay for our ads as they scale up, given that revenue coming in is always a couple of months behind the payment schedule up front?

It's human nature to plan for how things will work but not necessarily to plan for how they may *grow*. And what happens if a business grows unevenly? The implications of success can be quite different for each co-author within a partnership.

You and your co-writing partner should discuss the following and how they may be impacted by success.

- Can your systems for co-authoring a book be scaled up if needed?
- Can your systems for publishing a book be scaled up?
- How do you each define success?
- Is it possible to become too successful? What would that look like?
- Can your business systems (for tracking expenses and ad costs, etc.) scale up?
- Who would manage additional hired help?
- What if only one of the books in a shared, single-author series takes off?
- What if all but one author's book takes off?
- How do you feel about including new authors to your partnership to increase output?

How will you celebrate successes along the way?

Success looks different at different stages of the writing and publishing process. Too often we're aware of the bumps along the road but don't pay as much attention to the small but significant steps of progress we make.

Those who know us through The Creative Academy for Writers are aware that we're huge fans of champagne milestones. Celebrating mini wins supports you when times get challenging. We love planning our milestone celebrations.

We go out for dinner together (with the business paying!) to celebrate book releases and the achievement of specific income targets. And we often have mini bottles of champagne in the fridge so we can toast each other's successes. You'll know we've hit a specific income target when we host a writing retreat on the beach complete with cabana staff delivering fruity drinks with umbrellas.

When you have clear targets, you can set a budget that includes celebration.

Your Turn

- Journal about what wild success would look like for you. Imagine and write out what a typical day or week would be like in that successful world.
- What new challenges might success bring?
- Review systems and plans with your co-author to learn what would need to change if you were to expand.
- How will you and your partner celebrate success?

39

WHAT'S NEXT?

We know that over the course of this book, we've thrown you a lot of things to think about. As we mentioned in the beginning, you can dip in and out of it as needed and as your co-writing relationships evolve over time.

We find that as long we're knowledgeable about our own goals and motivations, realistic about where our skills lie, and diligent about checking in with each other regularly, our shared projects flow smoothly and are a wonderful addition to our writing careers.

We really hope you have just as much fun with your co-authored projects as we have with ours, and we'd love you to share your wins with us in The Creative Academy For Writers online community.

Your Turn

We've got a few last (optional, but appreciated!) Your Turn exercises for you before you're on your way.

1: Leave a review

We hope you found this book and the accompanying resources helpful. We'd be forever grateful if you took a moment right now to post a quick review wherever you bought your copy, and also on Goodreads and BookBub if you have accounts there.

Your review will help other writers find the book. It also shows us what you found most helpful. This book is part of a series, and your feedback will ensure our next books give you more of what you liked—so if you include in your review details of what you found most helpful, we'll take note!

2: Share with a friend

The only thing better than writing and reading books is sharing books with friends. If you know other writers who are interested in developing their writing into a full-time author career, please let them know you enjoyed this resource and found it helpful.

3: Join The Creative Academy for Writers

Having a community that understands what you're going through as a writer makes all the difference between getting stuck and getting it done. Join our fabulous free community at CreativeAcademyForWriters.com/join-us and get access to a wealth of our best resources.

4: Check out the other books in this series

It's always sad when you come to the end of a book. But the brilliant part about a series is that the fun doesn't *really* have to end! So put away your Kleenex. We've got more books in this series to help you along your writing and publishing journey. Be sure to check out our other titles on our website. You can find us at CreativeAcademyForWriters.com/books.

5: Check out the Strategic Authorpreneur podcast

For more great info on saving time, money and energy as you level up your writing career, check out the Strategic Authorpreneur Podcast at StrategicAuthorpreneur.com.

More Creative Academy Guides for Writers

We've got a whole series of books to help you along your writing and publishing journey.

Available in eBook & print

Scrappy Rough Draft by Donna Barker
Build Better Characters by Eileen Cook
Strategic Series Author by Crystal Hunt
Create Story Conflict by Eileen Cook
Full Time Author by Eileen Cook and Crystal Hunt
Create With Co-Authors by Donna Barker, Crystal Hunt and Eileen Cook

Come visit us…
www.CreativeAcademyForWriters.com

Want to access our collection of FREE courses and resources for writers? Visit us online at CreativeAcademyForWriters.com/resources.

ABOUT DONNA BARKER

Donna Barker spent twenty-five years as a ghostwriter for not-for-profit organizations before indie publishing her first novel. Realizing that having her name associated with her words wasn't as scary as she'd assumed, she gave up the ghost and has been publishing both non-fiction and romance (under the pen name Danika Bloom) ever since. Donna is a co-founder of The Creative Academy for Writers, where she helps members find joy with their motivation and accountability.

Donna lives hidden in the mountains near Vancouver, Canada. You can learn more about Donna's writing and work at DanikaBloom.com and DonnaBarker.com.

facebook.com/authordanikabloom
instagram.com/authordanikabloom

ABOUT CRYSTAL HUNT

Crystal Hunt is the author of over forty books in a variety of genres and formats. She writes non-fiction for authors as Crystal Hunt, contemporary romance as CJ Hunt, cozy mystery as Jean Hunt and children's books as Crystal Stranaghan (and a variety of other pen names). No matter what name  she's using, she is living her dream life as a full-time author and a founding mentor with The Creative Academy for Writers.

Crystal lives in Vancouver, Canada, with her husband. You can learn more about Crystal online at: CrystalHuntAuthor.com and RiversEndBookclub.com.

She's a bit of a hermit where social media is concerned, but if she *is* online, she can be found on Instagram.

instagram.com/cjhuntauthor

ABOUT EILEEN COOK

Eileen Cook is a multi-published, award-winning author with her novels appearing in nine languages. Her books have been optioned for film and TV. She spent most of her teen years wishing she were someone else or somewhere else, which is great training for a writer. She's an  instructor/mentor with The Creative Academy for Writers and Simon Fraser University's Writer's Studio program, where she loves helping other writers find their unique story to tell.

Eileen lives in Vancouver, Canada, with two very naughty dogs. You can learn more about her on her website at EileenCook.com or connect with her on social media.

facebook.com/EileenCook.author
twitter.com/Eileenwriter
instagram.com/eileencookwriter

ACKNOWLEDGEMENTS

We'd like to start off with a special thank you to all the authors who filled out our questionnaire about writing with co-authors!

Thanks to Mandy Eve-Barnett, Jim Jackson, Whitley Cox, Winona Kent, Shelley Adina, Adina Senft, Charlotte Henry, Roxanne Snopek, Regina Scott, C. A. Kinnee/Carol Kinnee, J. R. Thorn/Jennifer Thorn, Laura Greenwood, Stella and Audra Price, S. A. Price, Dagmar Avery (with K. Margaret), Anastasia Virgas, Jessi Honard, Marie Parks and the many, many others who are writing under secret pen names and filled out the survey anonymously.

Special thanks to Sofia Aves, Mia Harlan, Eva Delaney, Kat Parrish, and Stacey Wallace for sharing trade secrets from their successful co-author experiences.

Thanks to our editor, Amanda Bidnall, who makes us look good. (We take full responsibility for any errors introduced in layout and publication).

Stephanie Candiago, we greatly appreciate your help taking each project from manuscript to published and promoted book. Every co-author partnership needs a Stephanie to keep the team in line.

Thank you to the members of The Creative Academy for Writers, who are the community we always hoped to have, and to our personal friends and family, who support us when we spend our time writing these books.

RESOURCES

Books

The 12 Week Year: Get More Done in 12 Weeks than Others Do in 12 Months by Brian P. Moran and Michael Lennington, Wiley, 2013

5000 Words Per Hour by Chris Fox, Chris Fox Writes LLC, 2015

Amazon Ads for Authors: Tips and Strategies to Sell Your Books by Deb Potter, Fairytale Factory, 2020

Amazon Decoded by David Gaughran, 2021

Build Better Characters: The Psychology of Backstory & How to Use It in Your Writing to Hook Readers by Eileen Cook, The Creative Academy for Writers, 2019

Create Story Conflict: How to Increase Tension in Your Writing & Keep Readers Turning Pages by Eileen Cook, The Creative Academy for Writers, 2020

Deep Work: Rules for Focused Success in a Distracted World by Cal Newport, Grand Central Publishing, 2016

Emotional Intelligence: Why It Can Matter More than IQ by Daniel Goleman, Bantam Publishing, 2005

The Four Tendencies: The Indispensable Personality Profiles that Reveal How to Make Your Life Better (and Other People's Lives Better, Too) by Gretchen Rubin, Harmony, 2017

Full Time Author: How to Build, Grow and Maintain a Successful Writing Career that You Love by Eileen Cook and Crystal Hunt, The Creative Academy for Writers, 2021

Funny You Should Ask: Mostly Serious Answers to Mostly Serious Questions about the Book Publishing Industry by Barbara Poelle, Writer's Digest Books, 2020

Getting to Yes by Roger Fisher and William Ury, Penguin Books, revised edition 2011

Non-Fiction Book Proposals Anybody Can Write (rev.) by Elizabeth Lyon, Penguin Group, 2002

Let's Get Digital: How to Self-Publish, and Why You Should (fourth ed.) by David Gaughran, 2020

Personality Types: Using the Enneagram for Self-Discovery by Don Richard Riso, Mariner Books, 2003

Save the Cat Writes a Novel by Jessica Brody, Ten Speed Press, 2018

Scrappy Rough Draft: Use Science to Strategically Motivate Yourself & Finish Writing Your Book by Donna Barker, The Creative Academy for Writers, 2019

Strategic Series Author: Plan, Write and Publish a Series to Maximize Readership & Income by Crystal Hunt, The Creative Academy for Writers, 2019

Strategic Indie Publisher by Crystal Hunt and Stephanie Candiago, The Creative Academy for Writers, forthcoming in 2022

You Are a Badass at Making Money by Jen Sincero, Penguin Life, 2017

Co-written titles that we mention in this book

Barbarians at the Gate: The Fall of RJR Nabisco by Bryan Burrough and John Helyar, Harper Business, 2009

Black Book by James Patterson and David Ellis, Grand Central Publishing, 2018 (as an example of Patterson's shared style)

Blue Monday, Nicci French, Penguin Books, 2012

Everything I Needed to Know About Being a Girl I Learned From Judy Blume by Jennifer O'Connell, Meg Cabot and 20 other writers, Gallery Books, 2007

Freakonomics: A Rogue Economist Explores the Hidden Side of Everything by Steven D. Levitt and Stephen J. Dubner, HarperCollins Publishing, 2009

Good Omens by Neil Gaiman and Terry Pratchett, Corgi, 1991

Love Blooms by Elana Gray, C.C. Pine, Mia Harlan, Eva Delaney, Jewels Arthur, Hanleigh Bradley, and J.E. Cluney, independently published, 2021

Run Rose Run by Dolly Parton and James Patterson, Little, Brown and Company, March 2022

The Secret of the Old Clock by Carolyn Keene, Grosset and Dunlap, 1930 (as an example of the Nancy Drew Series)

The Talisman by Stephen King and Peter Straub, Gallery Books, 2018

The Three Musketeers by Alexandre Dumas, originally published in 1844

Websites, blogs and podcasts

Query Shark website by Janet Reid (QueryShark.blogspot.com)

Reedsy Blog: How to Write a Non-Fiction Book Proposal (Blog. reedsy.com)

Strategic Authorpreneur Podcast (StrategicAuthorpreneur.com)

Writing Excuses podcast "Barbie Pre-writing" (season 15, episode 29)

Lightning Source UK Ltd.
Milton Keynes UK
UKHW021047180522
403172UK00008B/777